CUL de SAC

Golden Treasury

by Richard Thompson

**Andrews McMeel
Publishing, LLC**
Kansas City • Sydney • London

Cul de Sac is distributed internationally by Universal Press Syndicate.

Cul de Sac Golden Treasury copyright © 2010 by Richard Thompson. All rights reserved. Printed in China. No part of this book may be used or reproduced in any manner whatsoever without written permission except in the case of reprints in the context of reviews. For information, write Andrews McMeel Publishing, LLC, an Andrews McMeel Universal company, 1130 Walnut Street, Kansas City, Missouri 64106.

10 11 12 13 14 WKT 10 9 8 7 6 5 4 3 2 1

ISBN-13: 978-0-7407-9152-9
ISBN-10: 0-7407-9152-4

Library of Congress Control Number: 2009943357

www.andrewsmcmeel.com

Introduction

In French, "cul-de-sac" means "bottom of the bag"; it's not a particularly nice phrase—the "bottom" part refers more to "your own personal rear end" kind of bottom. I didn't know this when I first thought of naming a comic strip set in the suburbs *Cul de Sac*. All I knew was that a cul-de-sac was a little dead-end turnaround popular in suburban developments, and that I thought I knew them well, having lived on several when I was growing up.

Since starting the strip, I've learned not only the French translation, but also the fact that cul-de-sacs (the dashes are more idiomatically correct) are now considered bad design in community planning; it's been found that they promote insularity, fail to foster a feeling of community, and are a wasteful, poor use of land. Also, they may contribute to childhood obesity. So, despite having a few early doubts, I couldn't have picked a better name for a comic strip.

Cul de Sac started as a weekly strip in the *Washington Post Magazine*. Some of these early strips have been included in this collection.

For Tom, Lee, and Greg, who made me do all this.

This drawing is a combination of the haunted, crazily leaning town from *The Cabinet of Dr. Caligari* and the huge wall from *King Kong*. I didn't realize this at the time I drew it, but the best ideas are often unintentional. And it makes perfect sense as I have always loved old horror movies.

"Bliss" is her first name, though I haven't yet discovered her last name. Sometimes you have to let your characters reveal themselves gradually, which is a nice way of saying that sometimes you have to wait until you can think of an appropriate funny name.

There were several versions of this. One had Beni saying, "Look, the Wild Things found Waldo! How grisly!" I kinda wish I'd kept that one in.

Most preschools don't have anything as formal as a back-to-school night for parents. This is just another sign of Blisshaven's forward-looking, progressive character, and Miss Bliss's delusions of grandeur, too.

Throughout the strip, Alice has a love-hate relationship with reading. Given the power of words, it's probably a healthy attitude, but I don't envy her future teachers.

That's probably Dill's mom warning Mrs. Otterloop about her juice mustache. It's the only time I've seen her.

Years ago, I read an interview with Maurice Sendak where he said that in Charles Dickens's books, everything is alive—every chair, spoon, door, the fire in the fireplace; everything jumps to life and has a personality. This is a logical extension of that. And you'll notice that the personality of the comic strip is snide and unlikeable.

Three car strips in a row. What can I say? Cars are fun to draw.

The rattiness of Alice's hair peaks in this strip. Maybe somewhere along the way, she grabbed a hairbrush.

The modern playground as a monster-sized digestive system. Another fun thing to draw!

Mr. Danders has a touching if overinflated estimation of his own personal accomplishments. And who can blame him? He deserves at least a BA.

Polyfill is based on a real toy that began life as a doggie chew toy.

Beni is based on my brother Tim, whose mechanical bent was apparent from about the age of three, when my mom had to pull him out from under a grocery store freezer unit where he'd crawled to find out how it made things cold. I think Tim had more talent with a hammer, though he wasn't necessarily trusted with one.

I can control bees with my mind!

I can't even control myself with my mind.

At Alice's age, I was almost convinced that I could control bees with my mind. Or at least offer them friendly advice.

Show us how you control bees with your mind.

BEE—

DO A LOOP-DE-LOOP.

Will you use your new-found power for good or evil?

Ah!

I'll spread it around to even things out.

Now make the bee do something useful.

BEE-GO FIX ME A BOLOGNA SANDWICH

BUZZ

RUN! RUN! RUN!

Hey, that's a june bug! Ha! Don't I feel silly.

No wonder it tried to sting us.

Timmy Fretwork is based on roughly five people. More recently in the strip, it's been revealed that he and Miss Bliss are an item, and that he's something of a jack of all trades, though he's not particularly adept at any of them. Several teachers of lower grades have told me that this is a frighteningly accurate portrayal of classroom behavior.

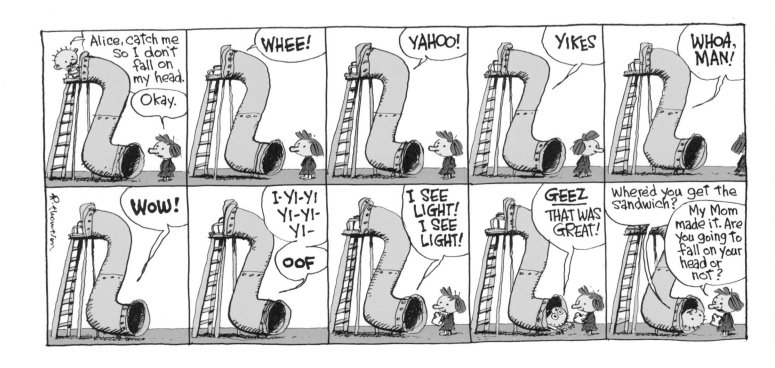

For today's feat of Bee Mind Control, I will attempt TWO BEES at once!

Kevin's dog found something really disgusting and he's <u>eating</u> it!

My 15 minutes are up, my star has dwindled, my fame has fled.

Where's this dog at?

R. Thompson

Look, they're digging for new houses.

Is that how they get new houses? Dig for them like potatoes?

I don't know. I'll go ask the guy wearing a hat.

Ok.

He patted me on the head and said I'm cute. He... he <u>tousled</u> my hair!

A sure sign of ignorance in an adult. He must not know either.

R. Thompson

Are you going to push me or <u>not</u>?

I can't reach you! The under-swing trench is too deep!

Go find me a taller kid then.

I can't get out! Help! I'm stuck in an under-swing trench!

R. Thompson

When I was small, we had solid, hard-packed dirt to stop our fall off playground equipment. Nowadays they've got cushioning beds of mulchy stuff that erodes easily, leaving the above-mentioned hazard to deal with. I ask you, which would you rather fall on?

This is the only glimpse so far of Dill's father. And no wonder.

Happy Birthday, Dill.

Hi, Alice! Here's your goodie bag.

Where is everybody?

They, um, they...

Did you give them their goodie bags and they all went home?

Uh-huh.

You confused them! You're supposed to give out the goodie bags LAST!

I'm not very good at this.

What do we do now?

Here's a birthday party game! I'll put a sticker on your head.

Why?

Now I'll put one on my head, and we'll ask questions to find out what's on them!

Okay. Why have you got a duck stuck on your head?

I don't know. What are you doing with a frog stuck on yours?

That was fun.

Wait, who won? The winner gets a plastic whistle.

It's usually a warning sign if I laugh at an idea I have. Chances are good that, on second glance, the humor that seemed so ingenious will have evaporated, leaving an empty and embarrassing shell of a joke. This one's an exception; it makes me laugh every time I read it. Now, having said that, I'm scared to read it again.

Alice! You're home already! How was Dill's party?

Awful.

Nobody else was there, the games were boring, his mom made his birthday cake a CARROT CAKE. Ick.

And look what's in the goodie bag — a little package of soy sauce, some frilly toothpicks and a teenie-weenie bottle of shampoo.

What are those things all over you?

Dill and I got into a sticker fight and I won! That part was great!

23

This sums up Alice pretty nicely in three action-packed and slightly gruesome panels. And I think having the ability to throw your own head in a fit of passion is a pretty universal yearning.

Quite a few of the Sunday strips from *Cul de Sac*'s first few years as a syndicated feature were redrawn versions of strips that originally ran in the *Washington Post Magazine*. Such as these two, for instance. The one below was a lot of fun to draw—all those variations on Alice's face from cubist to cloying. And in both, the action reaches its peak offstage, leaving the reactions afterward to carry the humor.

More fun with Alice's head (see two preceding pages). This seems like a pretty good example of my talent for depicting the thought process of a four year old. It's a facility that worries me more than a little.

I'm going like this for Halloween.

It says "Boo."

YAGH!

Four-year-olds shouldn't know about sarcasm.

MOM! HELP! YAGH!

R. Thompson

Petey, you're really going like that for Halloween?

Yes.

I don't want to dress up as something people will stare at.

And I don't like rubber masks. They smell and I can't see out of them.

If that's what he wants.

And yet he keeps asking to wear his viking helmet to school.

Halloween has almost more glamour for kids than Christmas, I think.

Don't get too far ahead, Alice.

I want everyone to see me!

NARA! What're you?

I'm Princess Fairyqueen!

R. Thompson

I already did all the houses on our street.

No! BUT! I'M! NO! BUT! I'M!

EEEE-YAGH!

Ooh! A scary monster!

Nara, being four and a half, is more sophisticated and accomplished than Alice, and she somewhat intimidates Alice.

Hey guys! How was trick or treating?

Awful.

Everybody thought I was Boo Radley. "Look! It's Boo Radley!" So finally I asked, "WHO'S BOO RADLEY?"

I felt like such a bonehead.

Aw, Petey...

I unwrapped most of my candy so it'll be faster to eat. Help me with the rest—

Why is our tree tied up?

So it won't jump out of the ground and chase you.

Oh.

When trees are young, they don't know how to stand still.

You can't get me! NYAA!

Taunting the inanimate is cruel.

I like the perspective of the sidewalk in the first two panels. It gives a nice visual "oomph," and it lets me cram all that stuff into the first panel in an interesting angle. Cramming stuff into little panels is, let's face it, the hardest part of drawing a newspaper comic strip.

I have to do a stupid leaf collection for preschool.

I kept the one I made in preschool.

Why?

I keep my entire output arranged by date. Here: "LEAF COLLECTION."

COUGH ~GAH~ DUST!

No! That was to be the centerpiece of my college admission!

Why do I have to make a Leaf Collection?

Miss Bliss wants you to learn about Nature and Shapes and Colors.

Do you know Shapes and Colors, Dad?

Of Course! I'm a grown-up!

What's the difference between a rhomboid and a parallelogram?

Well, Petey, that's a controversial subject—

AND WHO GIVES A **BIG FAT HOOT**, I wanna know.

You should thank me for helping you collect leaves.

Why does Miss Bliss make us do this stuff?

Leaves are boring.

HEY! A PIZZA COUPON!

Ooh! Put that in my Leaf Collection!

No. It doesn't count!

It'll be for extra credit! C'mon, Miss Bliss says thriftiness is good!

No! It's MINE! You owe me, Alice!

Did you help Alice with her Leaf Collection?

Yeah, and look! I found a pizza coupon!

Petey, that expired in August.

I know. I keep them.

You keep old coupons?

I have a binder full. It's labeled "Missed Opportunities."

If you watch her, Mrs. Otterloop is often doing odd chores: carrying things, fixing things, writing things—nothing too odd or weird, but nothing too easily identifiable. This is how I imagine a child views a parent: someone who's always busy at some activity that the child doesn't understand or much care about.

29

I am very pleased with everyone's Leaf Collection! They do Blisshaven Preschool PROUD!

You each get a star, a sticker and a leaf-shaped cookie!

WOW! I love leaf collecting!

I want to be a leaf collector!

I hear they drive GIANT VACUUM TRUCKS!

REALLY? Why wasn't that mentioned in the lesson plan?

Our class guinea pig is so cute!

But he never *does* anything.

Ah—

That is the way of the guinea pig. We respond to stimuli by becoming small lumps of inertia, implacable in our stillness.

R. Thompson

Tell me more of this "inertia." I like the sound of it.

I dunno. It smacks of the "bump-on-a-logism" my mom so roundly condemns.

Tell me more about guinea pigs.

Of course!

The Great Behemoth Guinea Pigs of the Ice Age would suddenly freeze, motionless, when attacked.

HEY!

Frustrated, the hunters would soon quit.

I don't feel challenged as a hunter-gatherer.

So you see, lethargy is often the best response.

I'm finally learning something in school!

R. Thompson

There's an ancient creation myth from some lost culture where a god has a little lump of leftover, unanimated clay, but he drops it and it rolls under a table where he can't get to it. He says, "$%^#, forget it; it's not worth the trouble." And then the lump wakes up and it's the first guinea pig.

The weaponizing of good intentions, which should be a subtitle for something.

Petey eventually becomes a master of the shoe-box diorama, effectively cramming all of human history into a space that's 12" x 7" x 4". Here he's just trying to think outside the box.

Maybe Dill has something to say and he'd like to hold the Talking Stick.

Yes, Miss Bliss!

HI, I'M MR. STICKY THE TALKING STICK! I'M SURE GLAD I'M NOT STILL GROWING OUT OF SOME STUPID TREE—

WITH A COUPLE OF STUPID BIRDS SITTING ON M—

GRAB

She took it away because "Mr. Sticky" is a dumb name.

PHOOEY.

I think this class still does not know the purpose of the Talking Stick.

The Talking Stick is about deference, respect and taking turns, the keys to civilized discourse.

Look! I made my own Talking Stick!

Me, too, out of a popsicle stick!

Mine has a ribbon!

Mine has a ribbon and glitter! So my Talking Stick is the loudest!

Alice, look. Here's how you can write your own name.

There! LS! It's like code for Alice!

REALLY? Let me try—

LS

I did it! HA HA HA!

Will just anyone be able to read this? Am I at risk of identity theft?

There's always that danger.

Interestingly, PT is code for Petey.

32

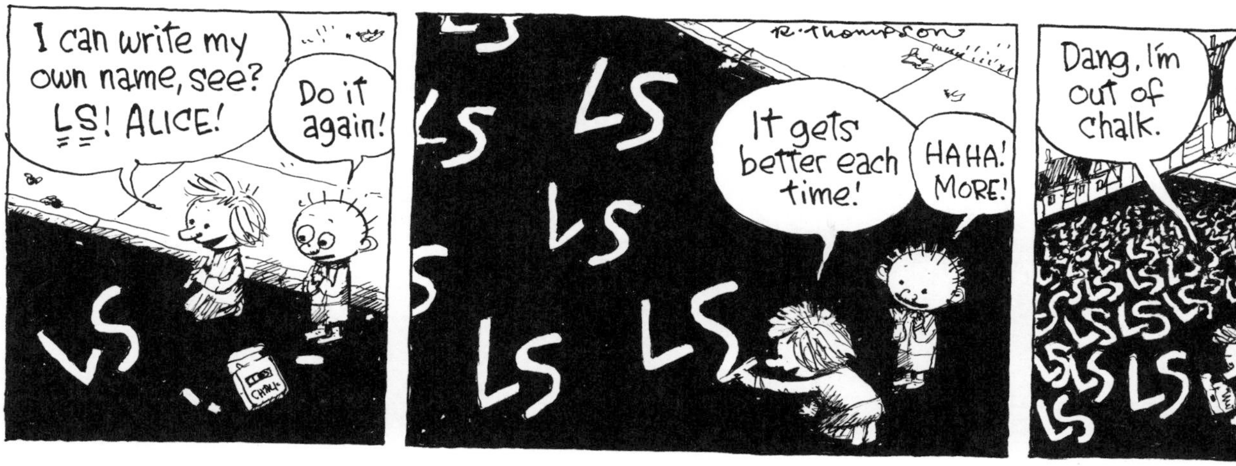
I can write my own name, see? LS! ALICE!
Do it again!
It gets better each time!
HA HA! MORE!
Dang, I'm out of chalk.
I think we're lost, too.

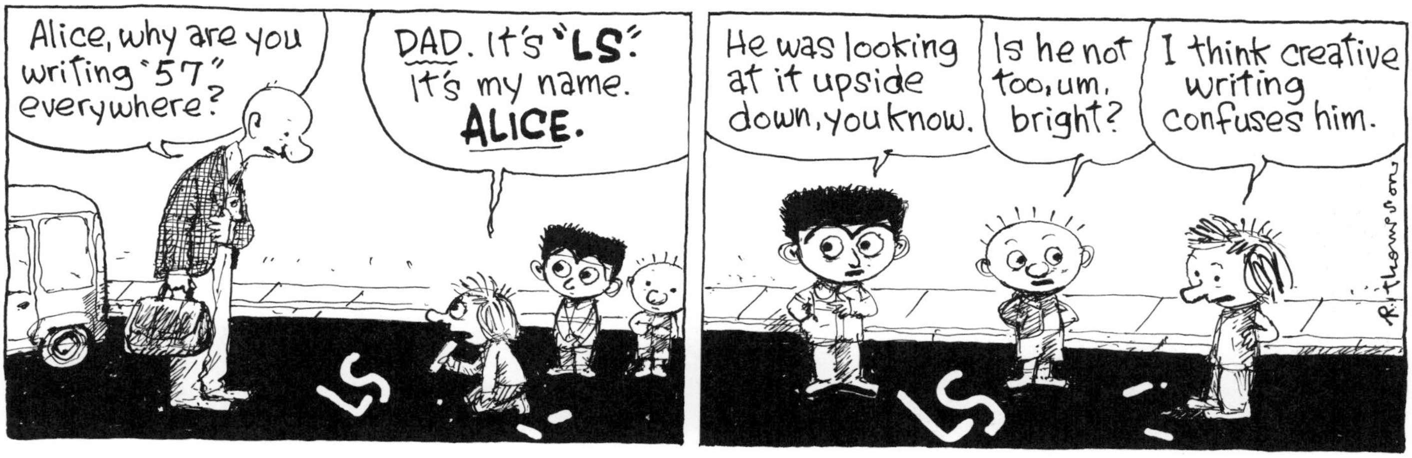
Alice, why are you writing "57" everywhere?
DAD. It's "LS." It's my name. ALICE.
He was looking at it upside down, you know.
Is he not too, um, bright?
I think creative writing confuses him.

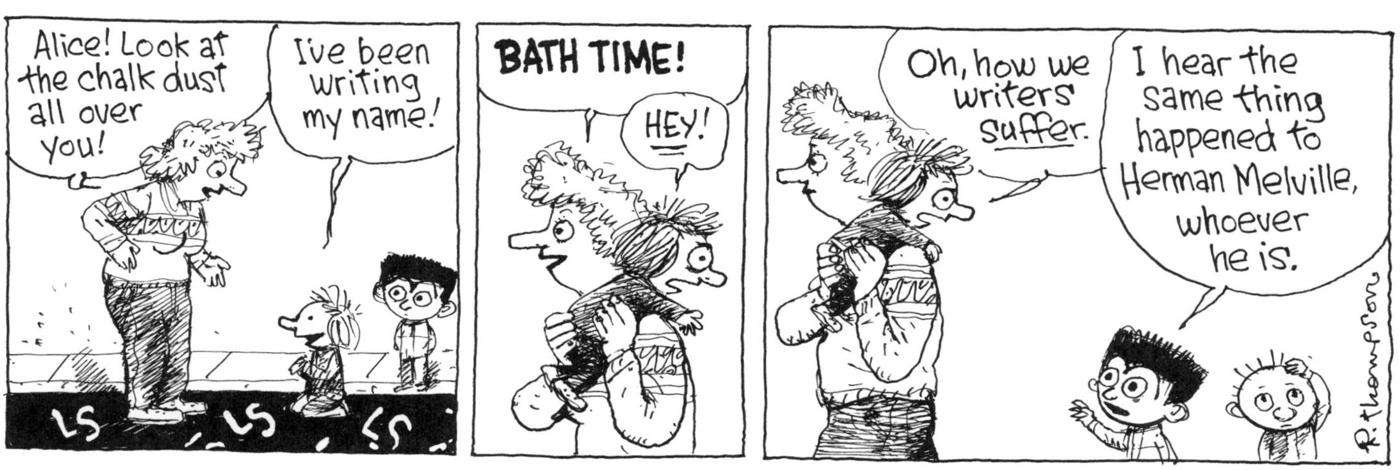
Alice! Look at the chalk dust all over you!
I've been writing my name!
BATH TIME!
HEY!
Oh, how we writers suffer.
I hear the same thing happened to Herman Melville, whoever he is.

We're going to my Grandma's for Thanksgiving.

She has a dog I'm scared of named Big Shirley.

Petey says Big Shirley probably ate Grandpa.

My grandma tells filthy jokes in Spanish.

Petey also says Grandma puts dog kibble in the stuffing.

My Grandma used to wave at traffic all day.

Then she got tired of traffic. Now she throws deviled eggs at it.

Grandma's got a good arm, too.

Grandma! It's us!

You people need a more distinctive car.

Grandma has lived so long with Big Shirley that she's gone a little feral.

Hi, Grandma! We're here for Thanksgiving Dinner!

Show her the food.

Look, Grandma! Food! FOOOOOD! We bring food! Friends!

Alice! Stop THAT!

You can come in, but those better not be beets.

Though I agree about the beets.

I once thought of adding two characters—a lawn gnome and a pink flamingo who ran a lawn service, only nobody wanted them anywhere near their lawns because lawn gnomes and pink flamingos are tacky. It's an idea that deservedly went nowhere, but it'd make a great animated movie. Hello, Pixar?

These two strips are related in that they mess around some with the comics form. In the strip above, Alice cannot be convinced that the cat strip is sequential. To her, it's all occurring simultaneously, in the here and now, which is appropriate for her character.

It's fun and interesting to play with time in a comic strip. Each panel is a minute slice of time, and the space between them can be nanoseconds or eons. Sometimes the space between the panels is more important than the panel itself. Which is a boon if you happen to be lazy about drawing.

The word "cheese" is comedy gold, at least among children. So is the word "pants." "Cheese pants" would be comedy gold of almost blinding brilliance.

Marcus DeMarco is an only child. He needs a sibling to siphon off some of his mom's high expectations.

Petey and food have an uneasy relationship. In fact, he's a world-ranking picky eater, and he's rather vain about it, too.

Winter hats such as Dill's do exist and are bought by parents who put them on their child's actual head. For this, I, as a cartoonist, am grateful.

Admit it—dealing with unknown babies can be awkward.

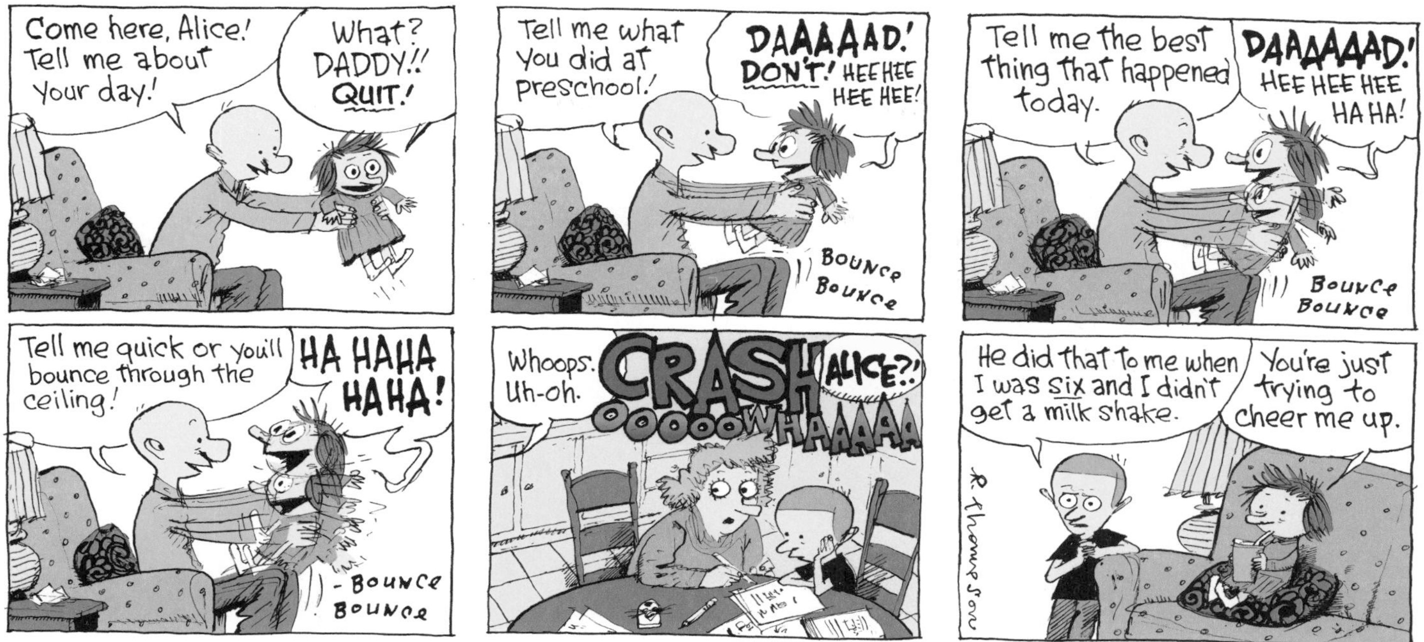
Come here, Alice! Tell me about your day!
What? DADDY!! QUIT!
Tell me what you did at preschool!
DAAAAAD! DON'T! HEE HEE HEE HEE!
BOUNCE BOUNCE
Tell me the best thing that happened today.
DAAAAAAD! HEE HEE HEE HA HA!
BOUNCE BOUNCE
Tell me quick or you'll bounce through the ceiling!
HA HAHA HAHA!
BOUNCE BOUNCE
Whoops. Uh-oh.
CRASH
ALICE?!
OOOOOWHAAAAA
He did that to me when I was six and I didn't get a milk shake.
You're just trying to cheer me up.
This strip provoked one of my first reader complaints. It came from a woman who thought Mr. Otterloop was being abusive. I thought he was merely being clumsy or, like Petey, awkward around those younger than him.

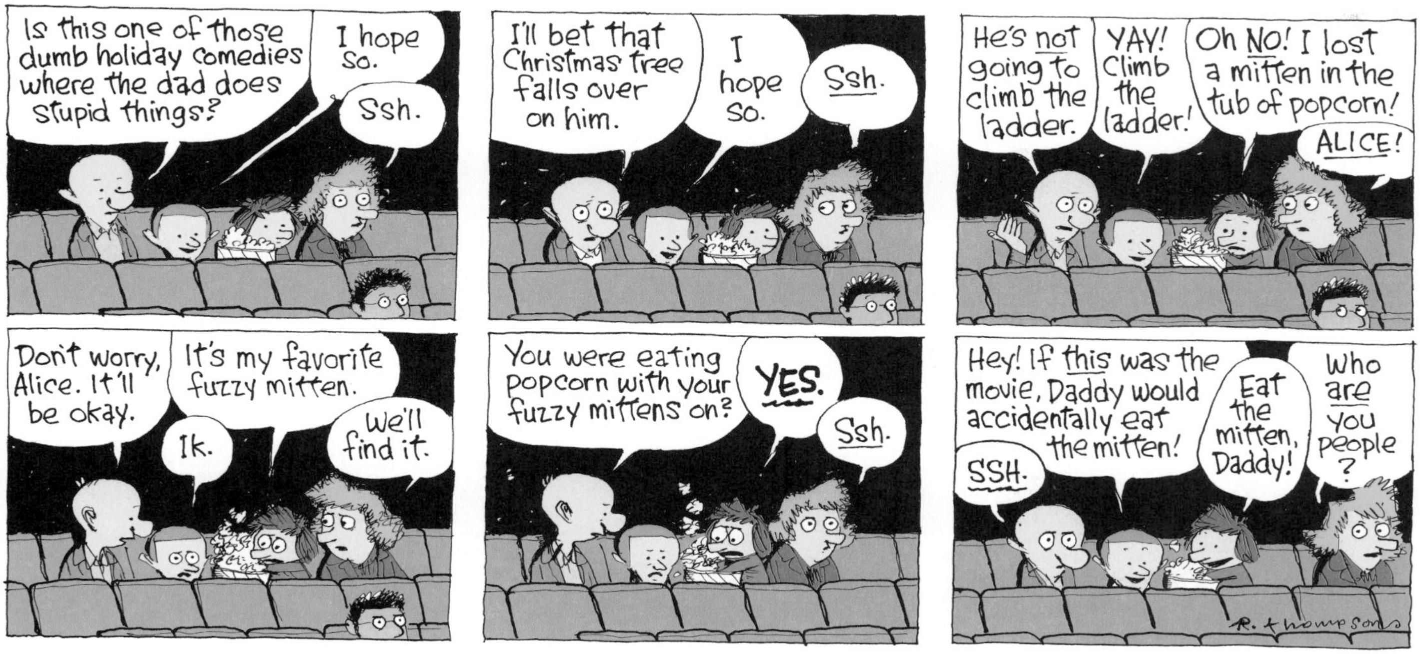
Is this one of those dumb holiday comedies where the dad does stupid things?
I hope so.
Ssh.
I'll bet that Christmas tree falls over on him.
I hope so.
Ssh.
He's not going to climb the ladder.
YAY! Climb the ladder!
Oh NO! I lost a mitten in the tub of popcorn!
ALICE!
Don't worry, Alice. It'll be okay.
It's my favorite fuzzy mitten.
Ik.
We'll find it.
You were eating popcorn with your fuzzy mittens on?
YES.
Ssh.
Hey! If this was the movie, Daddy would accidentally eat the mitten!
SSH.
Eat the mitten, Daddy!
Who are you people?
The man in the front row who gets annoyed and leaves was so compelling that someone sent me a fan-art drawing of him. Maybe I should focus on him instead of the Otterloops, but the enigma of his disappearance is what makes him interesting.

Babies and toddlers are rather malignant forces in *Cul de Sac*. So are grandmas. I can't account for this, but readers should complain.

Alice isn't a bad artist for a four year old.

This was drawn almost directly from life. Unfortunately, it was mine.

The largest Christmas sweater ever made was a forty-pound behemoth that featured lights, ornaments, tinsel, an animated nativity scene, dancing snowmen, and mixed choir and soloists. The unfortunate wearer had to be wheeled around like a parade float.

43

Inasmuch as the Otterloops live in a fairly new development, that shrub must predate their house.

44

Moms have sweaters; dads have hats.

Santa Claus commands a lot of awe and fear in children, even those that don't necessarily believe in him. So do clowns, but they don't have that religious/moral thing going on.

There's a weird pathos to unclaimed, lost, or unwanted toys, even those that are misguidedly educational, such as this one.

Please note Alice's feet-splayed sitting position, common among small children (though not adults, who can't do it). Just another example of the accuracy that *Cul de Sac* strives for every day.

Where'd you go for the holidays, guinea pig?

To the house of one of your classmates whose name escapes me.

His mother had "allergies", so I spent the entire week in the garage. It was awful: dark, cold and filled with thousands of ludicrous "handyman" gadgets.

R. Thompson

Whoops. I gotta go finish coloring something.

I'm thankful enough for the hospitality, but I still smell like a lawn mower.

Pop
Pop
POP
POP
Pop
Pop

Oh! Is that the new model?

Yes. I got it for Christmas.

Pop

Mine isn't as noisy. Have they improved it?

They increased the number of balls and they enlarged the spring! Isn't it sweet?

That was the most adult conversation I've ever had.

Wasn't it boring?

POP

R. Thompson

BOMP

Petey? Think fast.

ALICE! You're supposed to say that FIRST. REAL LOUD.

The finer points of sports elude me.

Did we win?

Throw it at him again and find out.

R. Thompson

48

Petey, what is New Year's? | It's when the year starts all over again. | All over again? Just like before? | No, it's new, so new things happen. | Everything starts new? EVERYTHING? | YES, Alice. | My name is now Sonia, and I'm an eight-foot-tall rabbit who's really cute. | Okey-dokey, Sonia.

It's New Year's, so everything is new, so I'm now a giant rabbit named Sonia. | We get to be something new? | Great! I'll be a grocery cart-herder! | I'll herd stray carts into long lines and push them around the parking lot. | I want to be that too! | We'll all be cart-herds! | We'll live at the grocery store and eat like kings!

Thus begins one of Dill's many minor obsessions.

We're going to be grocery cart-herds this year! | What? | We'll live at the grocery store and herd the stray carts into long lines! People will love us for it! | We'll have the run of the cereal aisle! | Oooh! | Will everyone please leave my room in a brisk yet orderly manner?

Once, in the parking lot of a big-box store, I saw a train of carts go by, towed by a small, beeping vehicle with flashing lights all over it. The head of every child present swiveled around to admire it, and those of most adults, too. The glamour of driving such a thing was overwhelming.

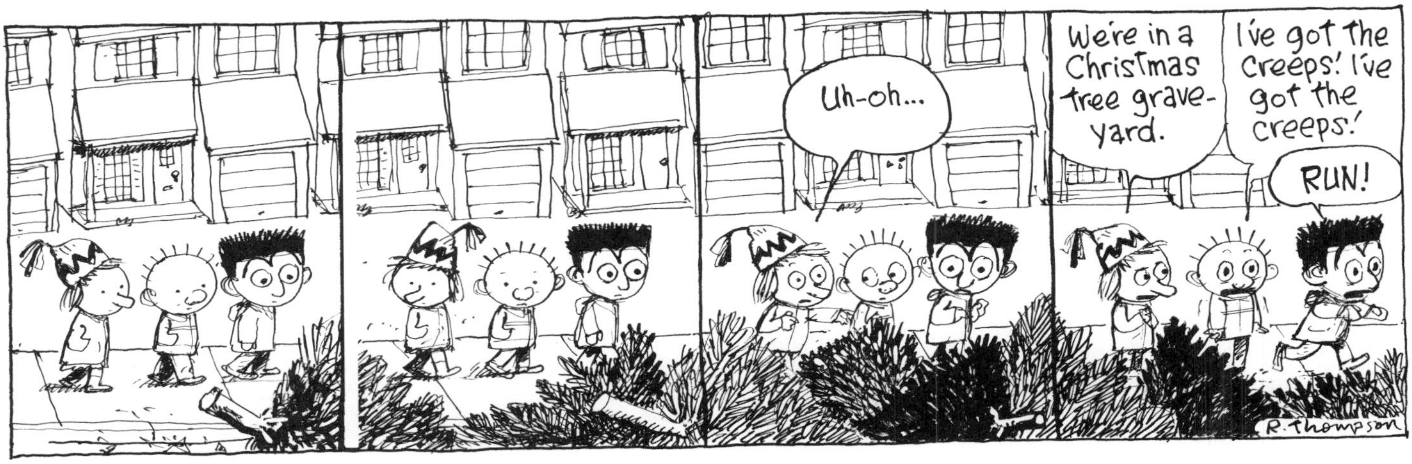
Uh-oh...
We're in a Christmas tree grave-yard.
I've got the creeps! I've got the creeps!
RUN!
R. Thompson

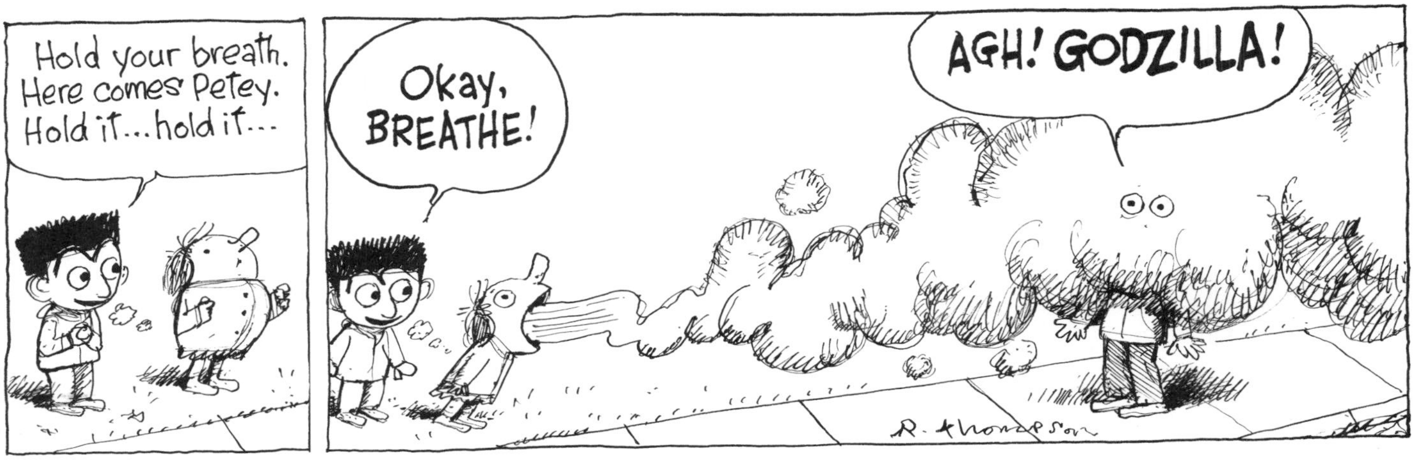
Hold your breath. Here comes Petey. Hold it... hold it...
Okay, BREATHE!
AGH! GODZILLA!
R. Thompson

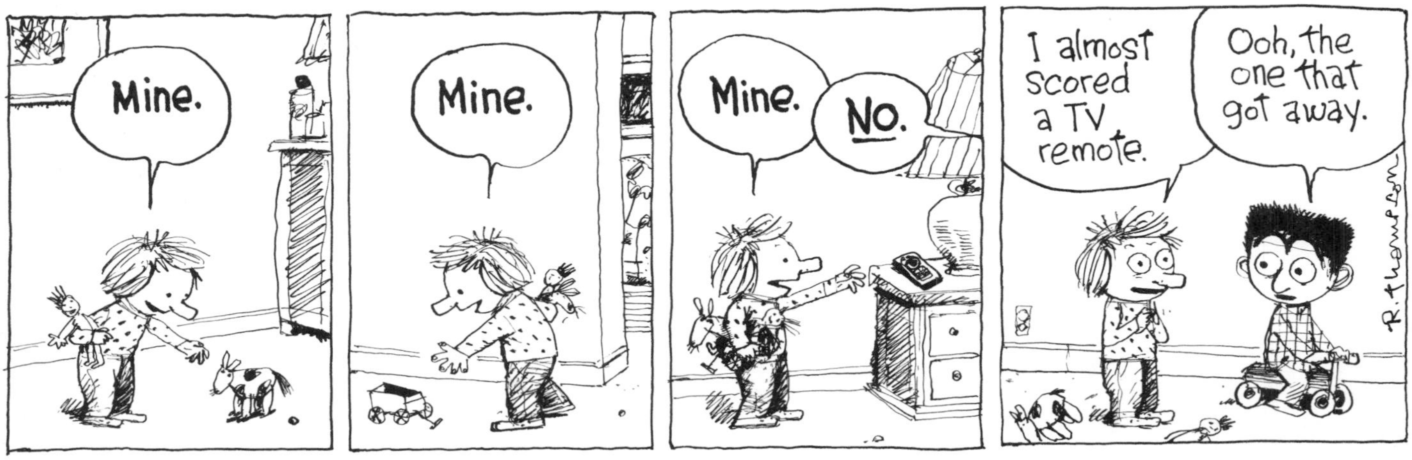
Mine.
Mine.
Mine.
NO.
I almost scored a TV remote.
Ooh, the one that got away.
R. Thompson

This pretty much sums up my whole view of family life. I could just stop right here and figure I've said enough and anything else is just an elaboration, but I won't.

No one ever calls Mr. Danders anything but "guinea pig," and I'm sure it annoys him no end. "Gweep" is as accurate as I could get in transcribing the noise that guinea pigs make.

These next twenty pages are a sampling of strips that ran in the *Washington Post Magazine*, where *Cul de Sac* began in 2004 as a Sunday-only feature. They were done in watercolor instead of the process color that is needed for most newspapers.

This launches one of several miniature epics where Danders escapes or is otherwise ejected from his cage.

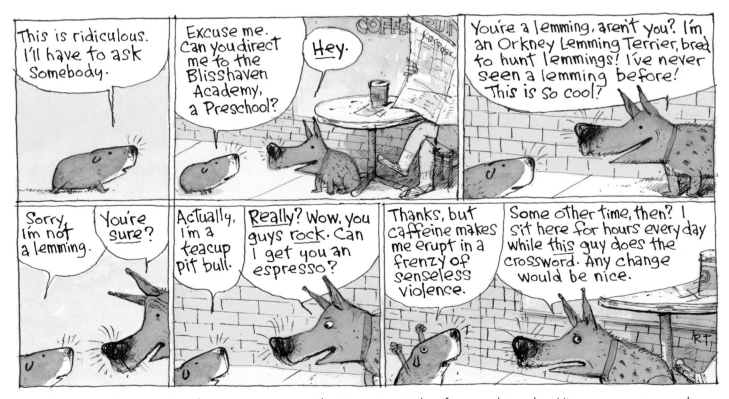

In each strip in the series, Danders assumes a new identity, or is mistaken for something else. His protean nature and knack for easy assimilation may be his greatest defenses. Or more likely, he's just so bland that nobody gives him much of a second glance.

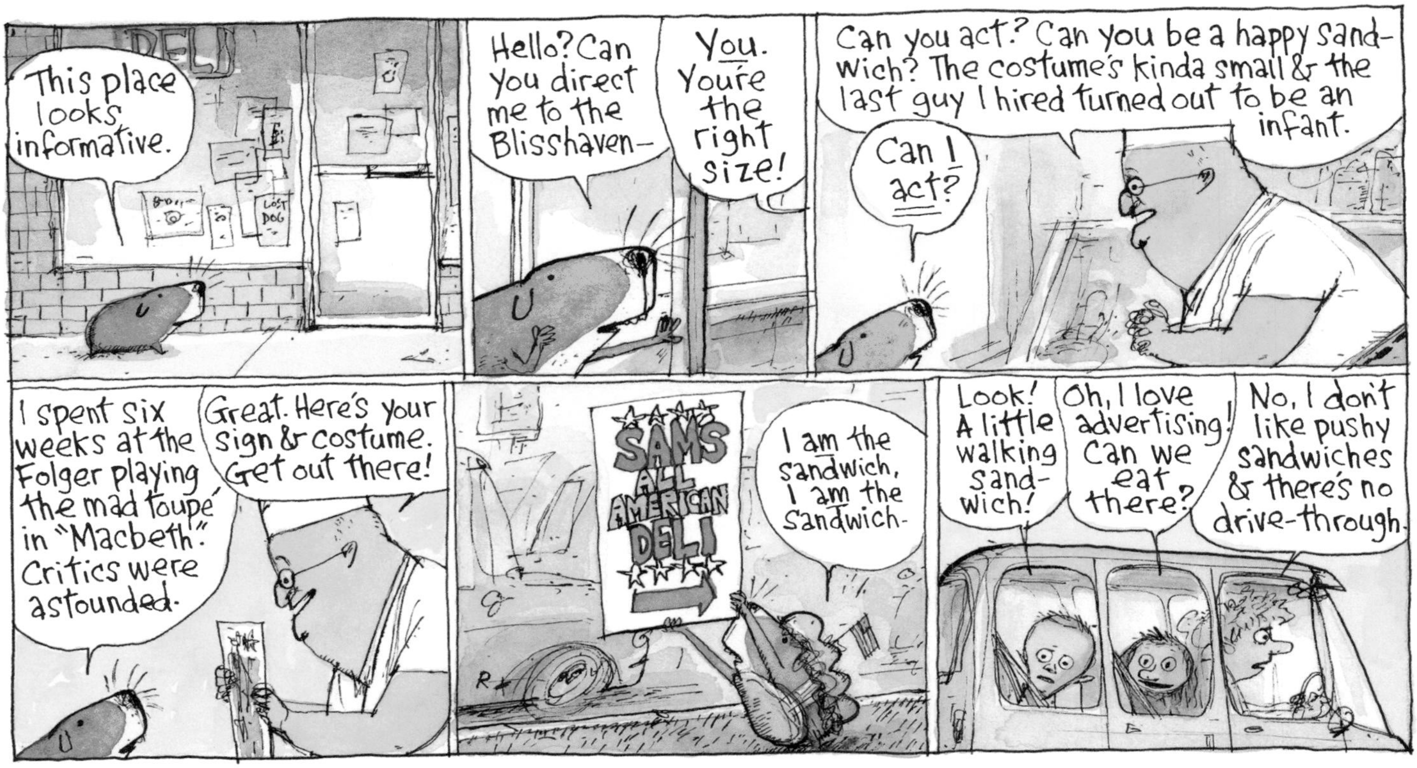
This place looks informative.
Hello? Can you direct me to the Blisshaven—
You. You're the right size!
Can you act? Can you be a happy sandwich? The costume's kinda small & the last guy I hired turned out to be an infant.
Can I act?
I spent six weeks at the Folger playing the mad toupé in "Macbeth". Critics were astounded.
Great. Here's your sign & costume. Get out there!
SAMS ALL AMERICAN DELI
I am the sandwich, I am the sandwich—
Look! A little walking sandwich!
Oh, I love advertising! Can we eat there?
No, I don't like pushy sandwiches & there's no drive-through.

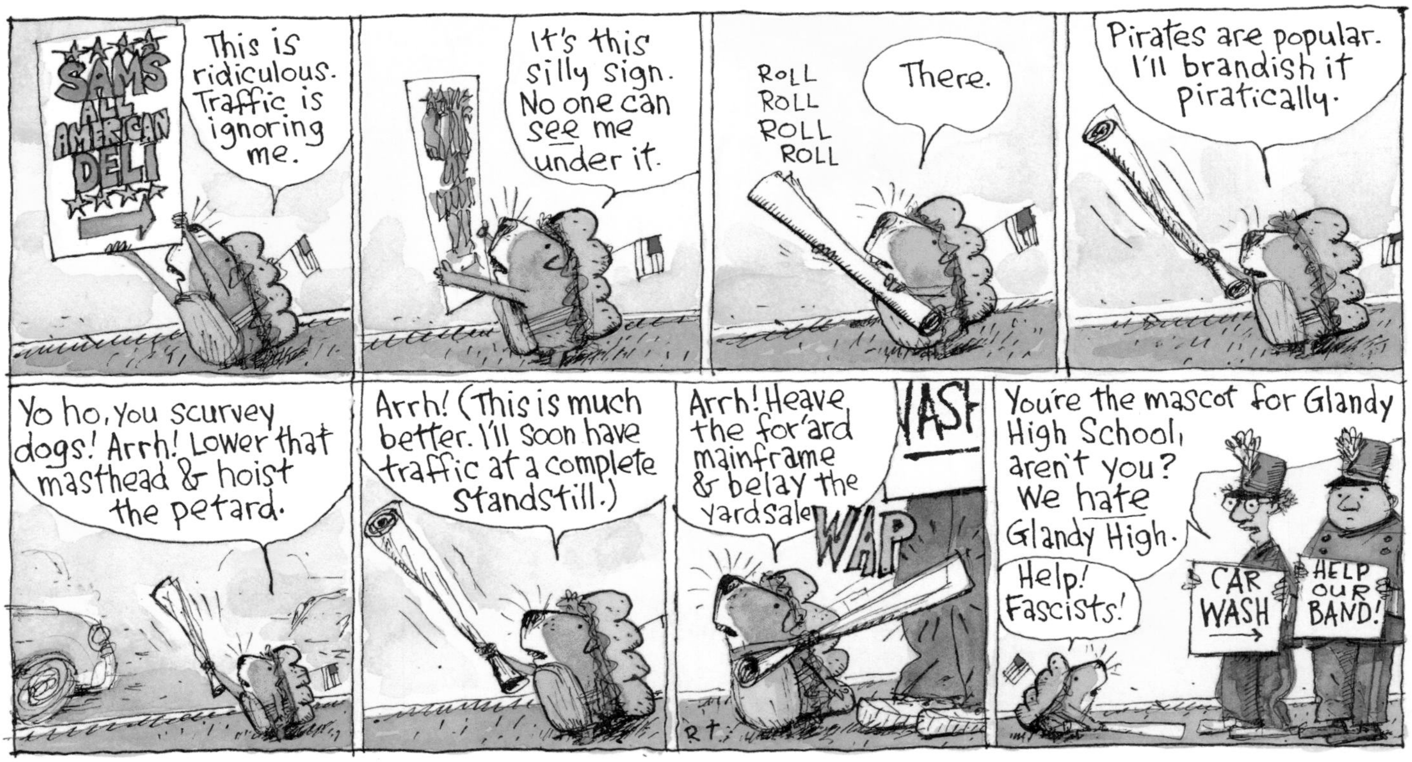
SAMS ALL AMERICAN DELI
This is ridiculous. Traffic is ignoring me.
It's this silly sign. No one can see me under it.
ROLL ROLL ROLL ROLL
There.
Pirates are popular. I'll brandish it piratically.
Yo ho, you scurvey dogs! Arrh! Lower that masthead & hoist the petard.
Arrh! (This is much better. I'll soon have traffic at a complete standstill.)
Arrh! Heave the for'ard mainframe & belay the yardsale
WASH
WAP
You're the mascot for Glandy High School, aren't you? We hate Glandy High.
Help! Fascists!
CAR WASH
HELP OUR BAND!

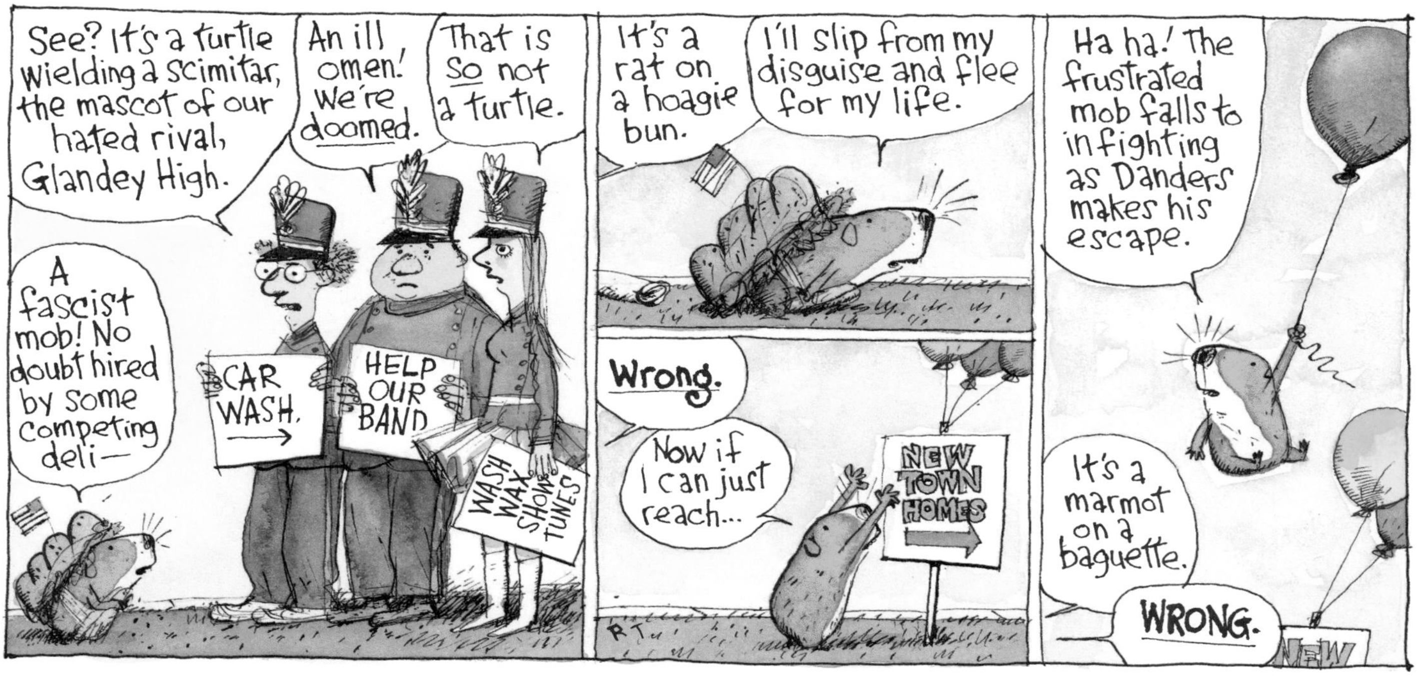
See? It's a turtle wielding a scimitar, the mascot of our hated rival, Glandey High.
An ill omen! We're doomed.
That is so not a turtle.
A fascist mob! No doubt hired by some competing deli—
CAR WASH
HELP OUR BAND
WASH WAX SHOW TUNES
It's a rat on a hoagie bun.
I'll slip from my disguise and flee for my life.
Wrong.
Now if I can just reach...
NEW TOWN HOMES
Ha ha! The frustrated mob falls to infighting as Danders makes his escape.
It's a marmot on a baguette.
WRONG.
NEW

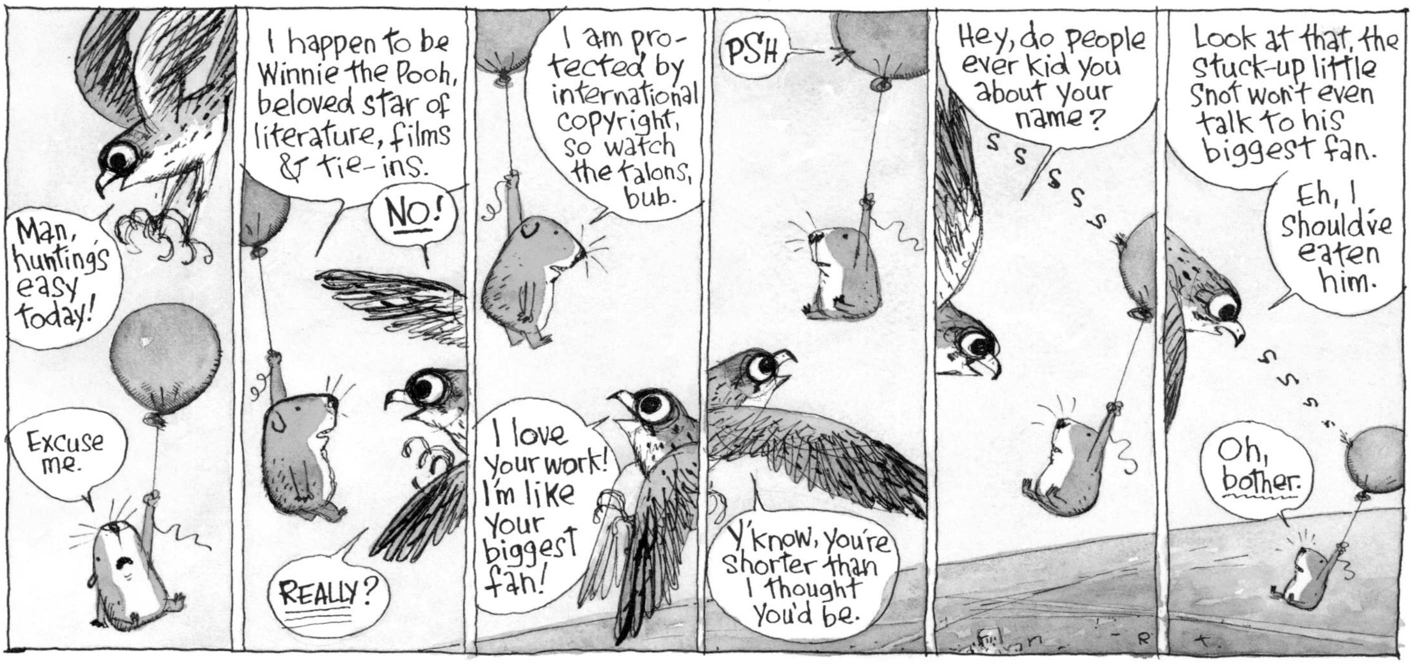
Man, hunting's easy today!
Excuse me.
I happen to be Winnie the Pooh, beloved star of literature, films & tie-ins.
NO!
REALLY?
I am protected by international copyright, so watch the talons, bub.
I love your work! I'm like your biggest fan!
PSH
Y'know, you're shorter than I thought you'd be.
Hey, do people ever kid you about your name?
S S S S S
Look at that, the stuck-up little snot won't even talk to his biggest fan.
Eh, I should've eaten him.
S S S S S
Oh, bother.

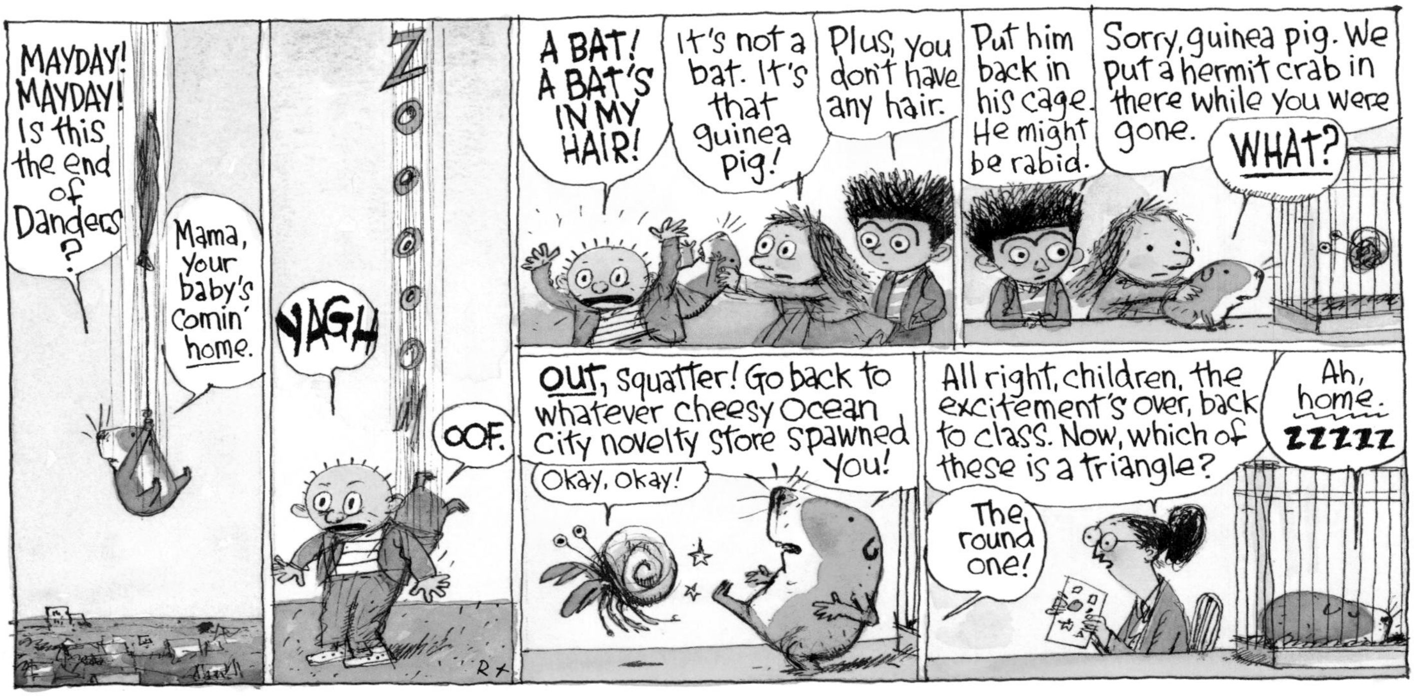
MAYDAY! MAYDAY! Is this the end of Danders?
Mama, your baby's comin' home.
Z
YAGH
OOF.
A BAT! A BAT'S IN MY HAIR!
It's not a bat. It's that guinea pig!
Plus, you don't have any hair.
Put him back in his cage. He might be rabid.
Sorry, guinea pig. We put a hermit crab in there while you were gone.
WHAT?
OUT, squatter! Go back to whatever cheesy Ocean City novelty store spawned you!
Okay, Okay!
All right, children, the excitement's over, back to class. Now, which of these is a triangle?
The round one!
Ah, home.
ZZZZZ

Wasn't that epic?

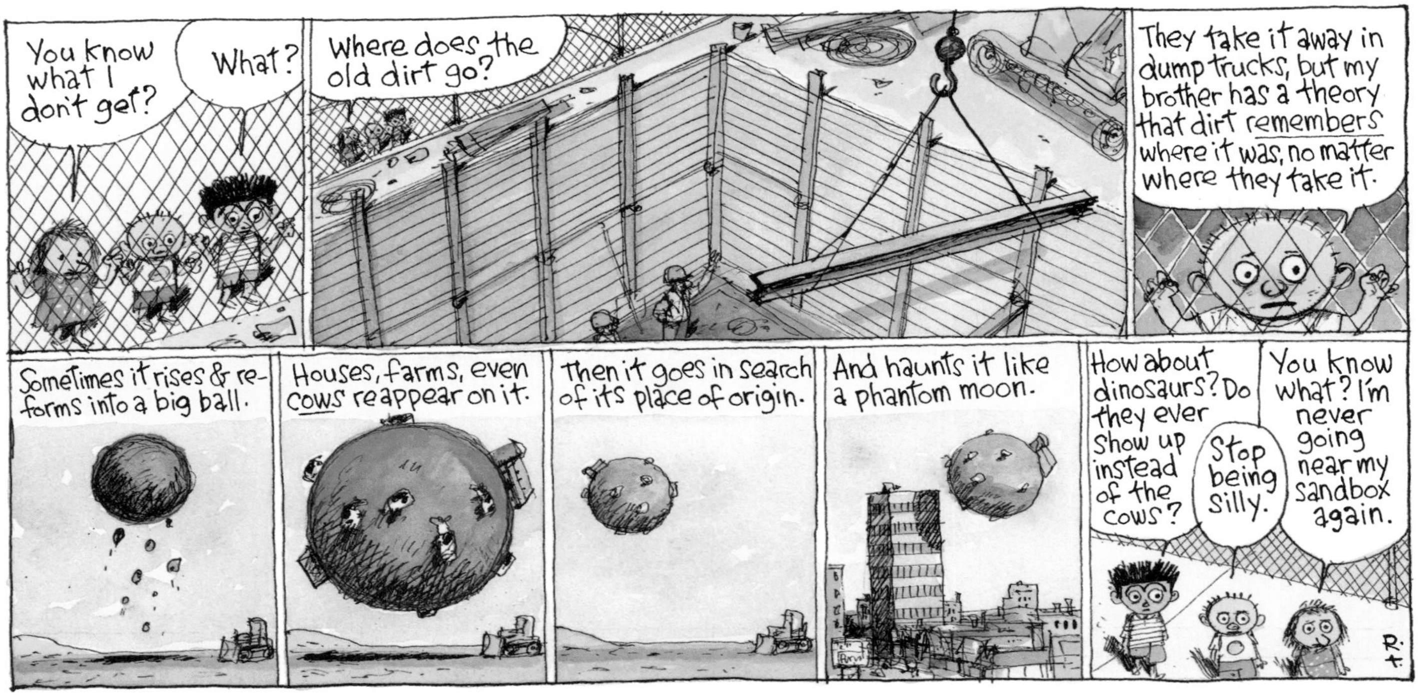
You know what I don't get?
What?
Where does the old dirt go?
They take it away in dump trucks, but my brother has a theory that dirt remembers where it was, no matter where they take it.
Sometimes it rises & re-forms into a big ball.
Houses, farms, even cows reappear on it.
Then it goes in search of its place of origin.
And haunts it like a phantom moon.
How about dinosaurs? Do they ever show up instead of the cows?
Stop being silly.
You know what? I'm never going near my sandbox again.

For years, I lived close enough to the county fairgrounds that I could hear the tractor pulls and demolition derbies (I couldn't quite smell the livestock though). Please note the cow-tipping gag.

I salute you, *Family Circus!*

Many people can do actual creative work in a coffee shop, which impresses me as glamorous and bohemian. I can't; I'm easily distracted and I can barely think straight if there's another person in the room. And as for sketching in a public place, forget it. I hate to admit it, but the prospect of being caught in a creative act mortifies me.

Another Danders epic, this one a comic tragedy of love and loss.

FedUPS struck me as hugely funny when I thought of it four or five years ago. I'm still waiting for a laugh, and it's probably too late. I'm sure it's been independently thought of hundreds of times by now by other, funnier people. Sometimes, if I think of something like this that strikes me as hugely funny and original, I'll type it into Google and discover thousands of hits.

Please note the knuckle tattoos.

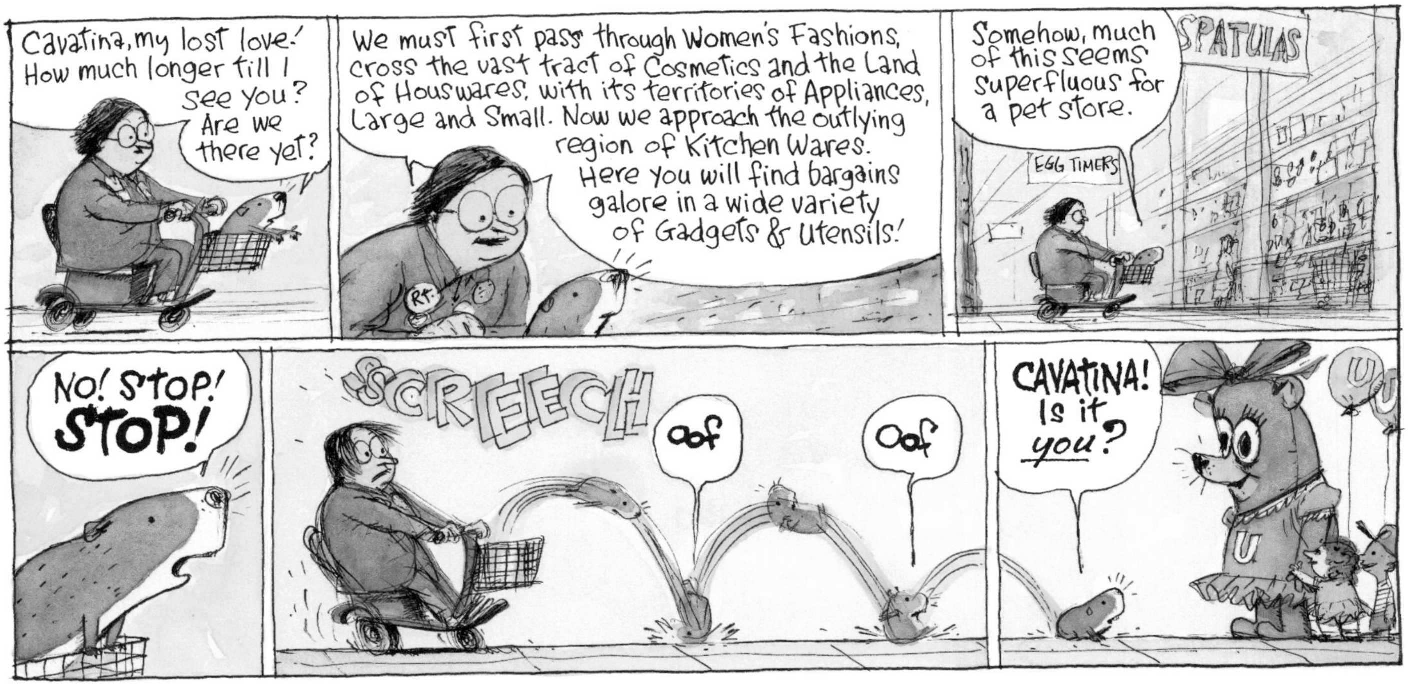

Cavatina, my lost love! How much longer till I see you?
Are we there yet?
We must first pass through Women's Fashions, cross the vast tract of Cosmetics and the Land of Houswares, with its territories of Appliances, Large and Small. Now we approach the outlying region of Kitchen Wares. Here you will find bargains galore in a wide variety of Gadgets & Utensils!
Somehow, much of this seems superfluous for a pet store.
SPATULAS
EGG TIMERS
NO! STOP! STOP!
SCREECH
oof
Oof
CAVATINA! Is it you?

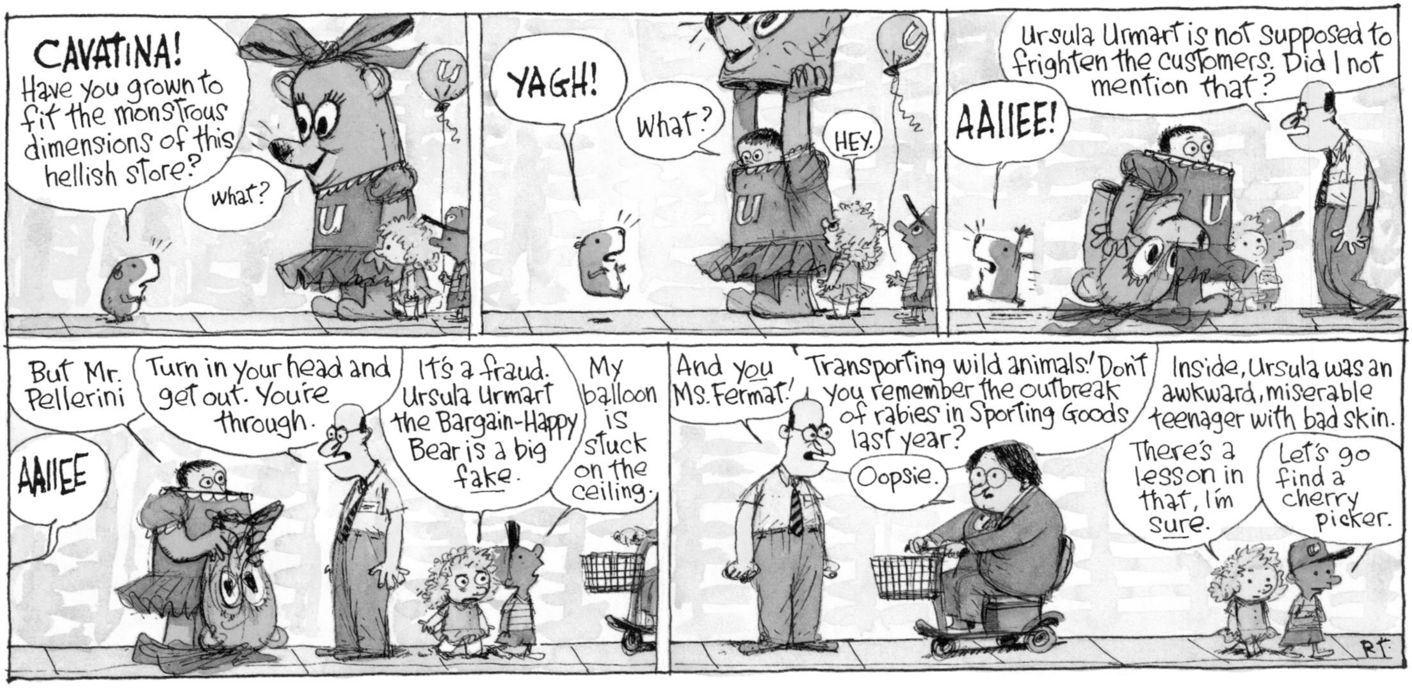

CAVATINA! Have you grown to fit the monstrous dimensions of this hellish store?
what?
YAGH!
What?
HEY.
AAIIEE!
Ursula Urmart is not supposed to frighten the customers. Did I not mention that?
But Mr. Pellerini
Turn in your head and get out. You're through.
AAIIEE
It's a fraud. Ursula Urmart the Bargain-Happy Bear is a big fake.
My balloon is stuck on the ceiling.
And you Ms. Fermat!
Transporting wild animals! Don't you remember the outbreak of rabies in Sporting Goods last year?
Oopsie.
Inside, Ursula was an awkward, miserable teenager with bad skin.
There's a lesson in that, I'm sure.
Let's go find a cherry picker.

That was epic, too, wasn't it?

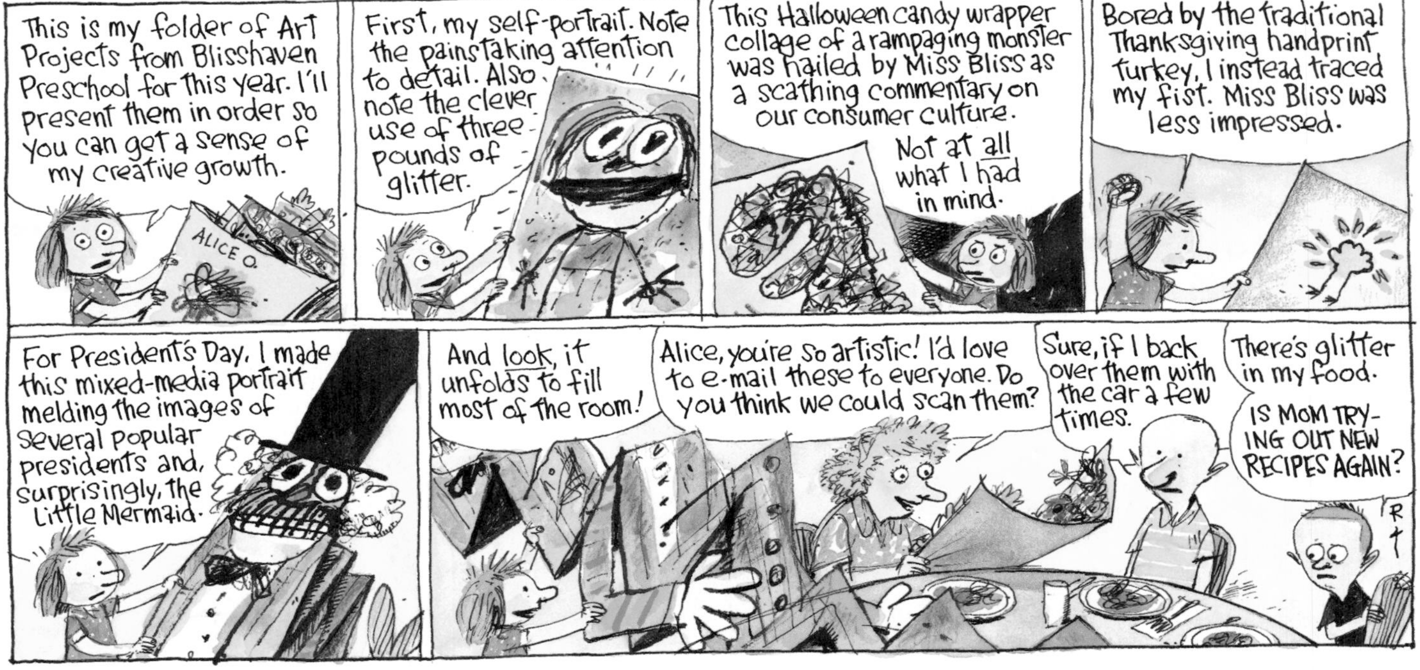
This is my folder of Art Projects from Blisshaven Preschool for this year. I'll present them in order so you can get a sense of my creative growth.
ALICE O.
First, my self-portrait. Note the painstaking attention to detail. Also note the clever use of three pounds of glitter.
This Halloween candy wrapper collage of a rampaging monster was hailed by Miss Bliss as a scathing commentary on our consumer culture.
Not at all what I had in mind.
Bored by the traditional Thanksgiving handprint turkey, I instead traced my fist. Miss Bliss was less impressed.
For President's Day, I made this mixed-media portrait melding the images of several popular presidents and, surprisingly, the Little Mermaid.
And look, it unfolds to fill most of the room!
Alice, you're so artistic! I'd love to e-mail these to everyone. Do you think we could scan them?
Sure, if I back over them with the car a few times.
There's glitter in my food.
IS MOM TRYING OUT NEW RECIPES AGAIN?
RT

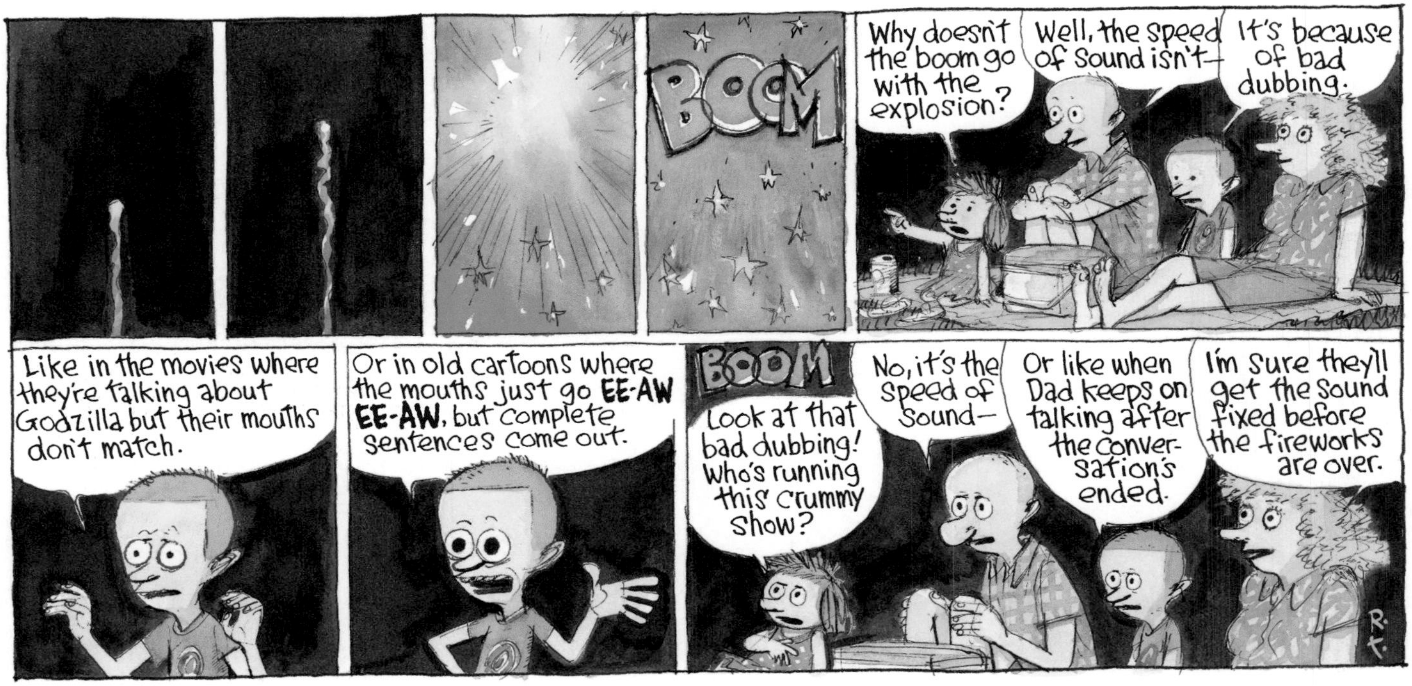
BOOM
Why doesn't the boom go with the explosion?
Well, the speed of sound isn't—
It's because of bad dubbing.
Like in the movies where they're talking about Godzilla but their mouths don't match.
Or in old cartoons where the mouths just go EE-AW EE-AW, but complete sentences come out.
BOOM
Look at that bad dubbing! Who's running this crummy show?
No, it's the speed of sound—
Or like when Dad keeps on talking after the conversation's ended.
I'm sure they'll get the sound fixed before the fireworks are over.
R.T.

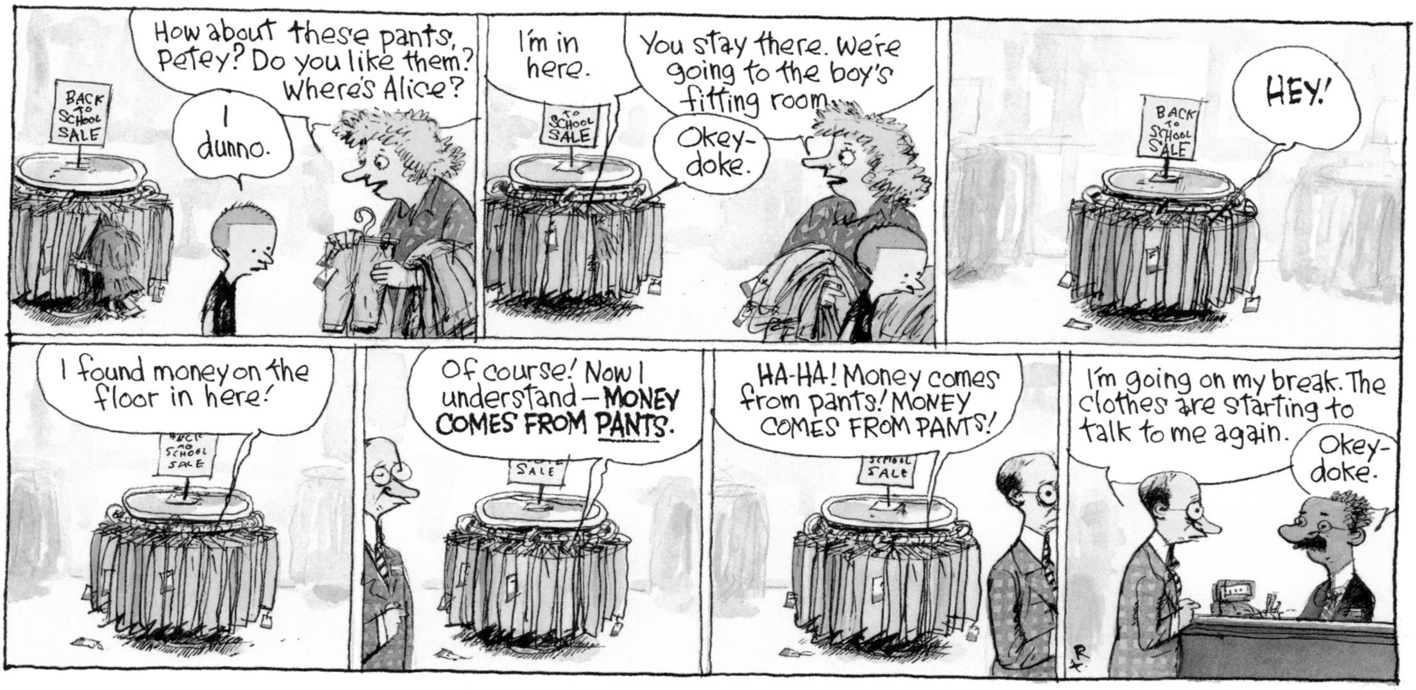
How about these pants, Petey? Do you like them? Where's Alice?
BACK TO SCHOOL SALE
I dunno.
I'm in here.
You stay there. We're going to the boy's fitting room.
TO SCHOOL SALE
Okey-doke.
BACK TO SCHOOL SALE
HEY!
I found money on the floor in here!
Of course! Now I understand—MONEY COMES FROM PANTS.
HA-HA! Money comes from pants! MONEY COMES FROM PANTS!
I'm going on my break. The clothes are starting to talk to me again.
Okey-doke.

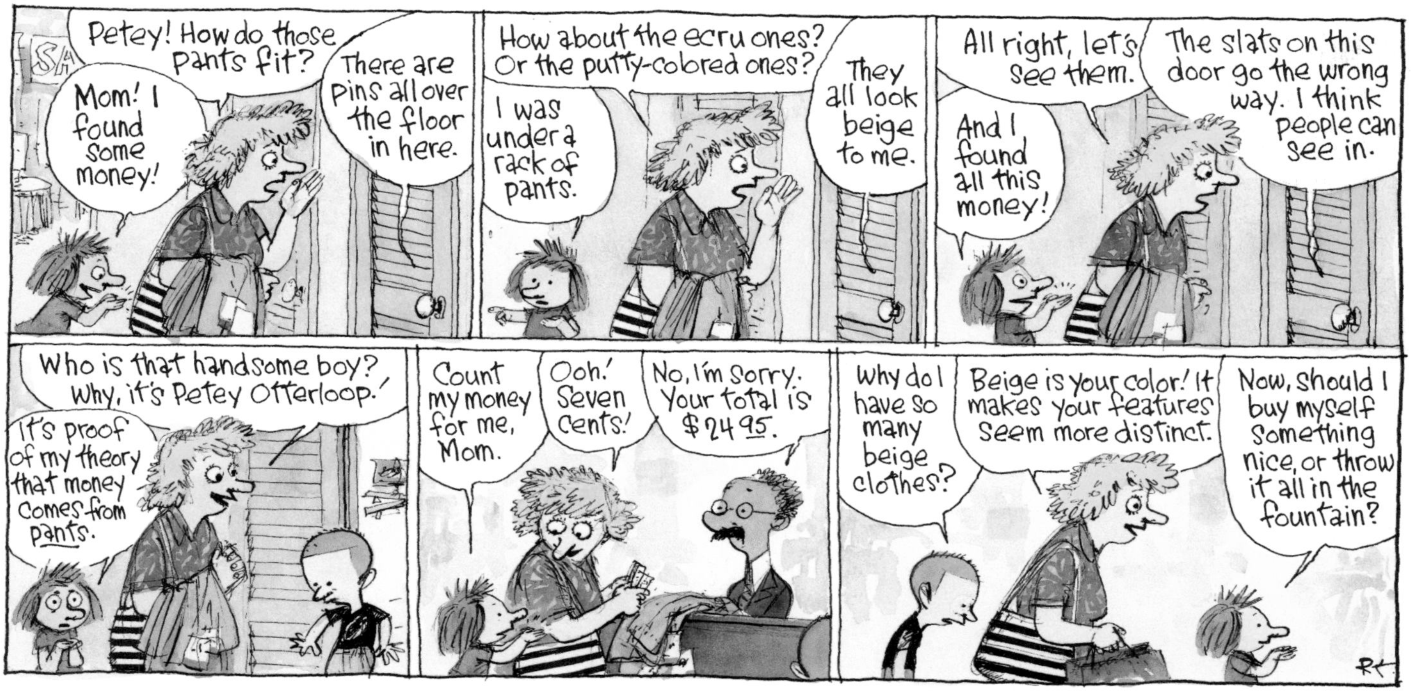
Petey! How do those pants fit?
Mom! I found some money!
There are pins all over the floor in here.
How about the ecru ones? Or the putty-colored ones?
I was under a rack of pants.
They all look beige to me.
All right, let's see them.
And I found all this money!
The slats on this door go the wrong way. I think people can see in.
Who is that handsome boy? Why, it's Petey Otterloop!
It's proof of my theory that money comes from pants.
Count my money for me, Mom.
Ooh! Seven cents!
No, I'm sorry. Your total is $24.95.
Why do I have so many beige clothes?
Beige is your color! It makes your features seem more distinct.
Now, should I buy myself something nice, or throw it all in the fountain?

This is Ernesto Lacuna, Petey's sort-of friend who may be imaginary (more on that later). His name is a pun on the great Cuban composer Ernesto Lecuona and the word "lacuna," which means "gap or missing section." OK, so maybe that's a little too clever, but it fits him; he's kind of an enigma, and kind of a James Bond villain in embryo. I haven't decided whether he is imaginary or not, and I don't think I ever will.

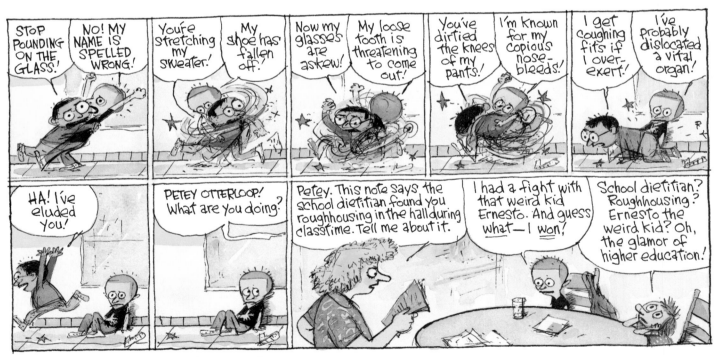

A passive-aggressive fistfight strikes me as funny.

I grew up around Washington, D.C., and *Cul de Sac* was originally more explicitly set there. This kind of encounter is pretty common, especially the name-forgetting part.

In the earlier version of *Cul de Sac*, Petey played the trombone, but I changed it to the oboe when it went into syndication. The trombone was funny as it's loud and demonstrative, with all that elbow-throwing slide action; it was therefore counterintuitive for Petey, who aims to be unobtrusive. But trombones are hard to draw, so it's "Hello, oboe!"

I salute you, Lemony Snicket.

The habit of turning all sentences into questions by ending them with a rising inflection is called "uptalking." Small children do it, and adults, too, to provoke a response and ensure that they're being paid attention to. It's probably a sign of insecurity.

This is a very accurate depiction of a DC Metro train, and of how I would act if I suddenly bellowed "pufferbellies" into a cell phone.

Eskimos actually only have a few words for "snow," like the man said. The notion that they had lots of words for it has a lot of charm though.

This little adventure is drawn almost directly from life, alas.

Nara was called "Narjeel" for a while, maybe because of a slipup on her registration form.

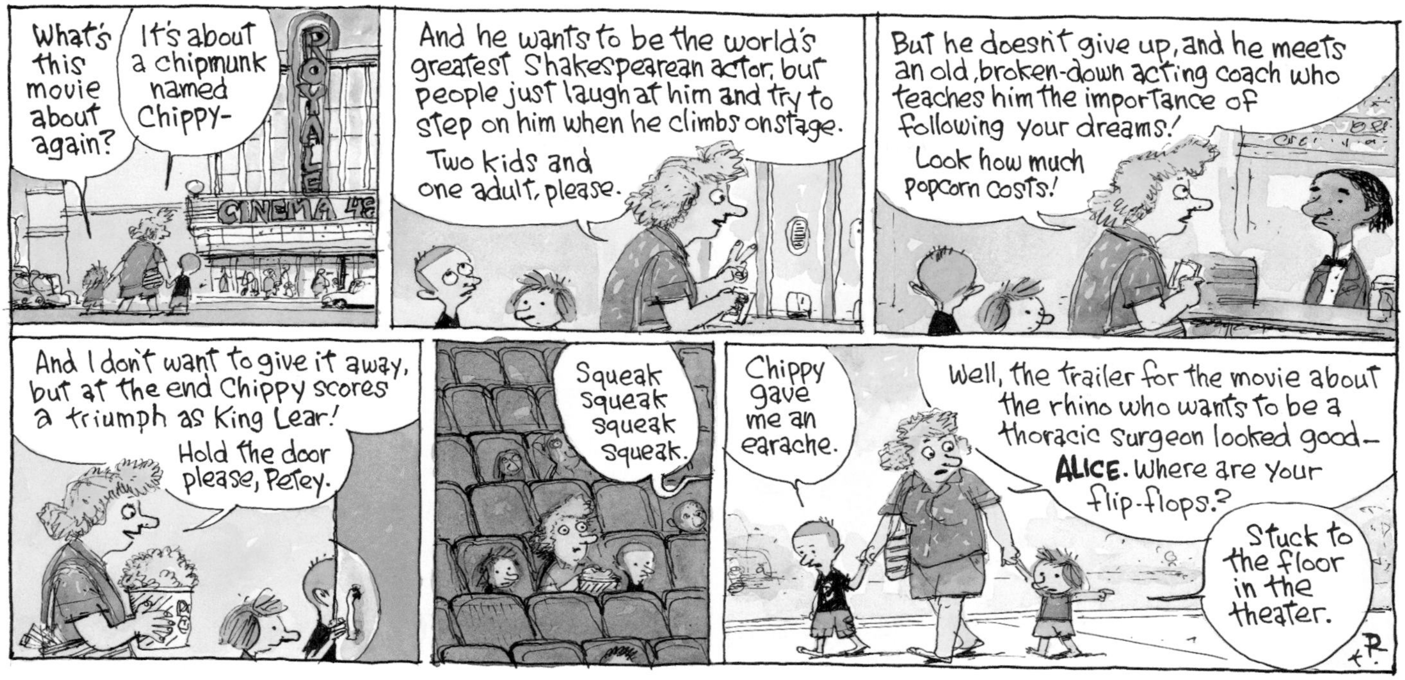
What's this movie about again?
It's about a chipmunk named Chippy-
ROYALE
CINEMA
And he wants to be the world's greatest Shakespearean actor, but people just laugh at him and try to step on him when he climbs onstage.
Two kids and one adult, please.
But he doesn't give up, and he meets an old, broken-down acting coach who teaches him the importance of following your dreams!
Look how much popcorn costs!
And I don't want to give it away, but at the end Chippy scores a triumph as King Lear!
Hold the door please, Petey.
Squeak squeak squeak squeak.
Chippy gave me an earache.
Well, the trailer for the movie about the rhino who wants to be a thoracic surgeon looked good— **ALICE.** Where are your flip-flops?
Stuck to the floor in the theater.

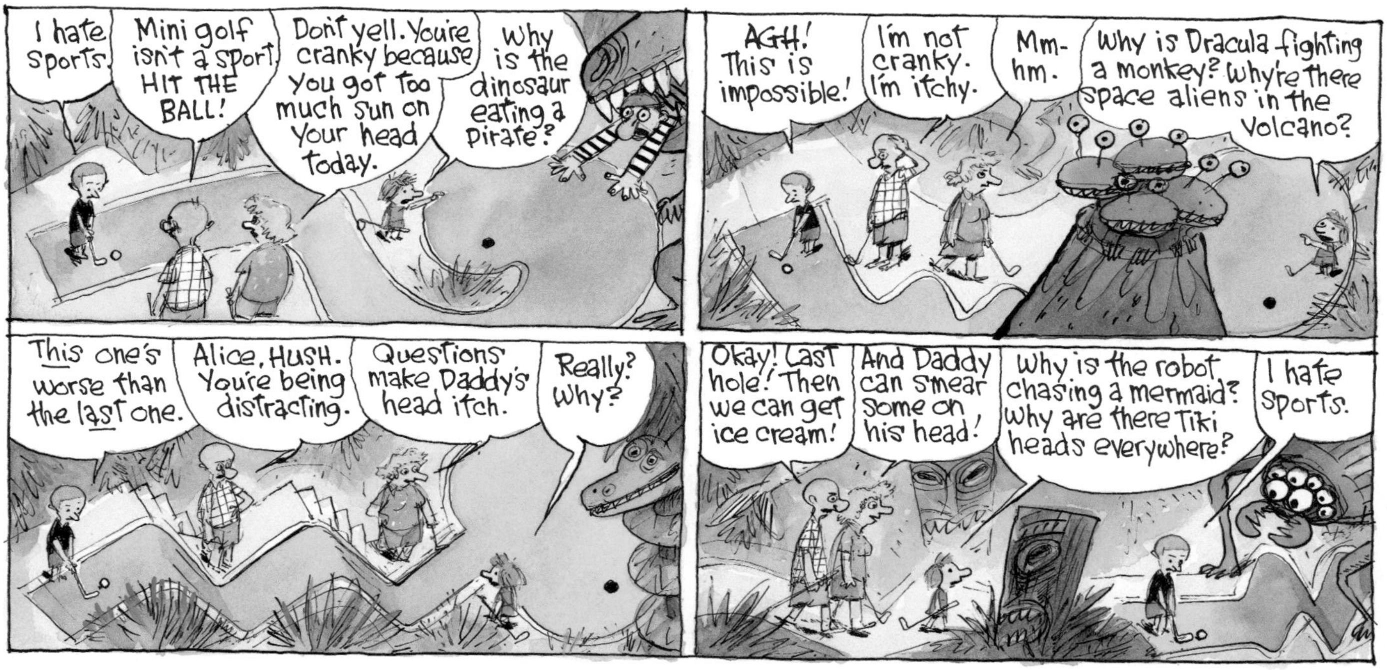
I hate sports.
Mini golf isn't a sport. HIT THE BALL!
Don't yell. You're cranky because you got too much sun on your head today.
Why is the dinosaur eating a pirate?
AGH! This is impossible!
I'm not cranky. I'm itchy.
Mm-hm.
Why is Dracula fighting a monkey? Why're there space aliens in the volcano?
This one's worse than the last one.
Alice, HUSH. You're being distracting.
Questions make Daddy's head itch.
Really? Why?
Okay! Last hole! Then we can get ice cream!
And Daddy can smear some on his head!
Why is the robot chasing a mermaid? Why are there Tiki heads everywhere?
I hate sports.

Among them, Dill's numerous brothers possess almost all the skills known to man, many of dubious legality.

Speaking of skills, nose blowing is a learned skill, and not an easy one.

Daddy, read me the book about the duck.

OK, Alice, if that'll make you feel better.

The duck loses his favorite hat, it's blue, so he goes all over asking everyone, have you seen my hat, it's blue, and the cow says no, and the pig says no, and the dog says no, **so** the duck goes home and closes the door and there's the hat on the back of the door!

Well, you just told me the whole story.

But I like watching your chin wiggle around when you read it.

Mrs. Otterloop, I've made a get-well card for Alice.

Dill! That's very nice of you!

Today at preschool, since Alice stayed home, nobody yelled, nobody threw dirt at recess, nobody hogged all the crayons. It was the most boring day ever.

Would you like to go see her?

If Alice ever learns not to grab toys away from me, I hope to marry her someday.

Hi, Dill.

Hi, Alice. I made a get-well card for you. See?

It's a giant germ stomping on your head!

It's the nicest card I've ever gotten that didn't have money in it.

Remember that in 20 years when I ask you to marry me.

Dill's a pretty good artist for a four year old.

Random self-absorption—a sure sign of four-year-oldism.

That Time-Out Corner seems to see a lot of visits by group tours.

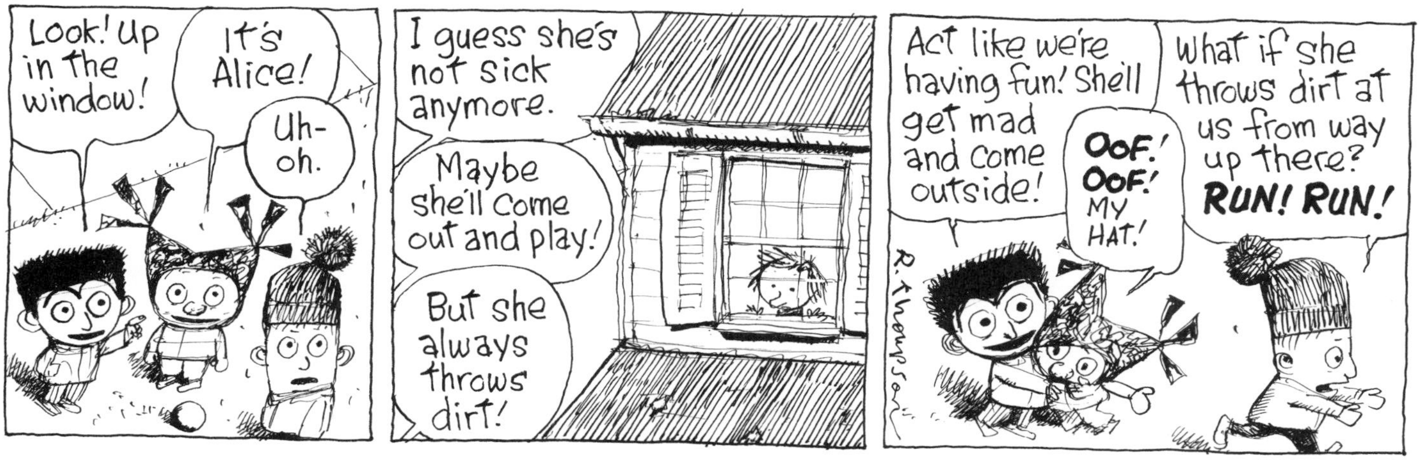
Look! Up in the window!
It's Alice!
Uh-oh.
I guess she's not sick anymore.
Maybe she'll come out and play!
But she always throws dirt!
Act like we're having fun! She'll get mad and come outside!
OOF! OOF! MY HAT!
What if she throws dirt at us from way up there? **RUN! RUN!**
R. Thompson

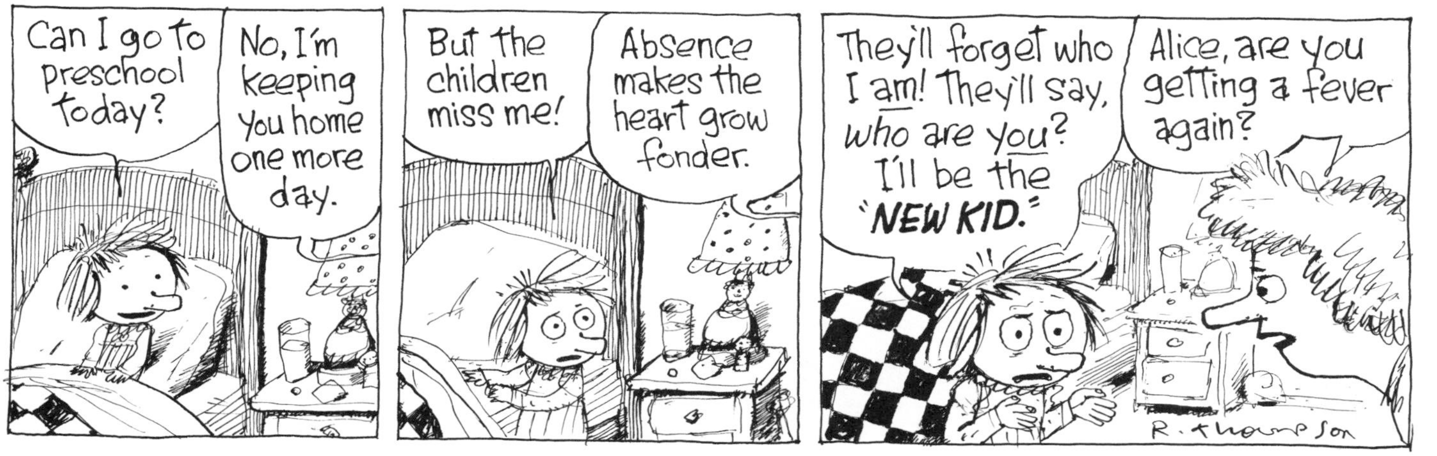
Can I go to preschool today?
No, I'm keeping you home one more day.
But the children miss me!
Absence makes the heart grow fonder.
They'll forget who I am! They'll say, who are you? I'll be the "**NEW KID.**"
Alice, are you getting a fever again?
R. Thompson

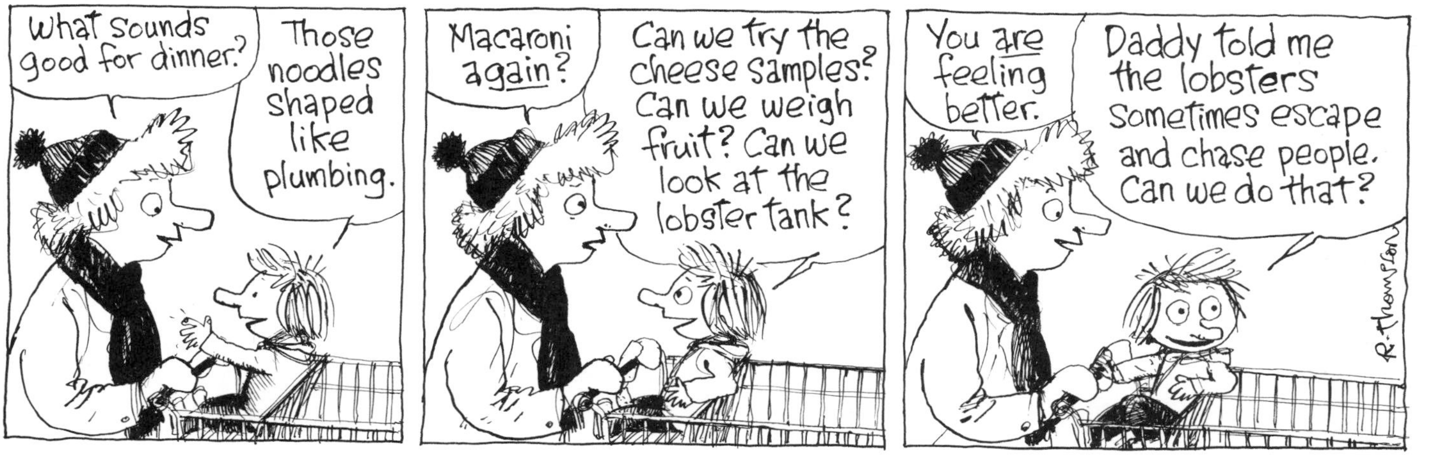
What sounds good for dinner?
Those noodles shaped like plumbing.
Macaroni again?
Can we try the cheese samples? Can we weigh fruit? Can we look at the lobster tank?
You are feeling better.
Daddy told me the lobsters sometimes escape and chase people. Can we do that?
R. Thompson

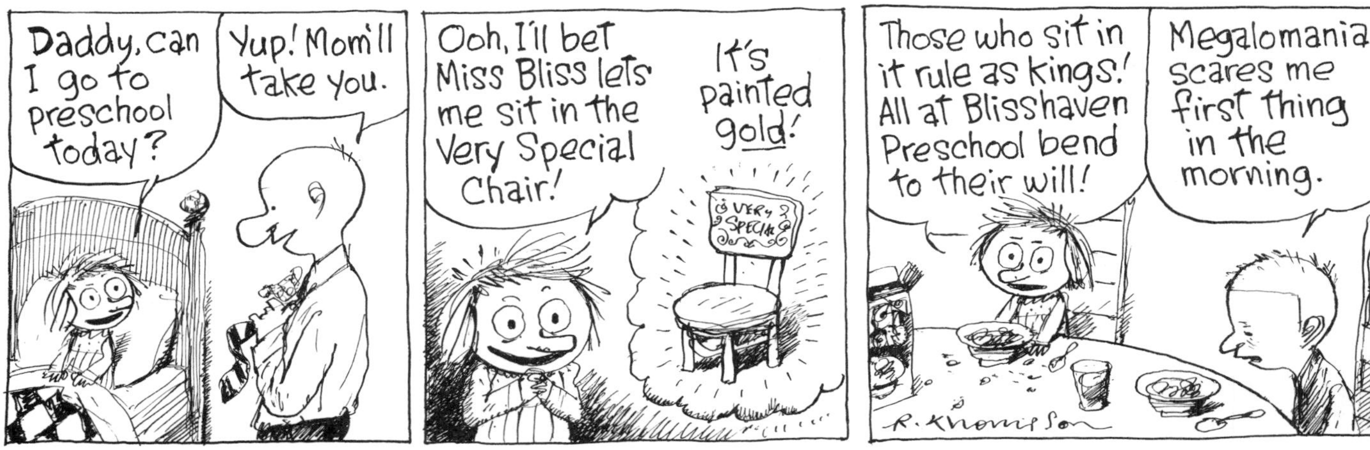
Daddy, can I go to preschool today?
Yup! Mom'll take you.
Ooh, I'll bet Miss Bliss lets me sit in the Very Special Chair!
It's painted gold!
VERY SPECIAL
Those who sit in it rule as kings! All at Blisshaven Preschool bend to their will!
Megalomania scares me first thing in the morning.

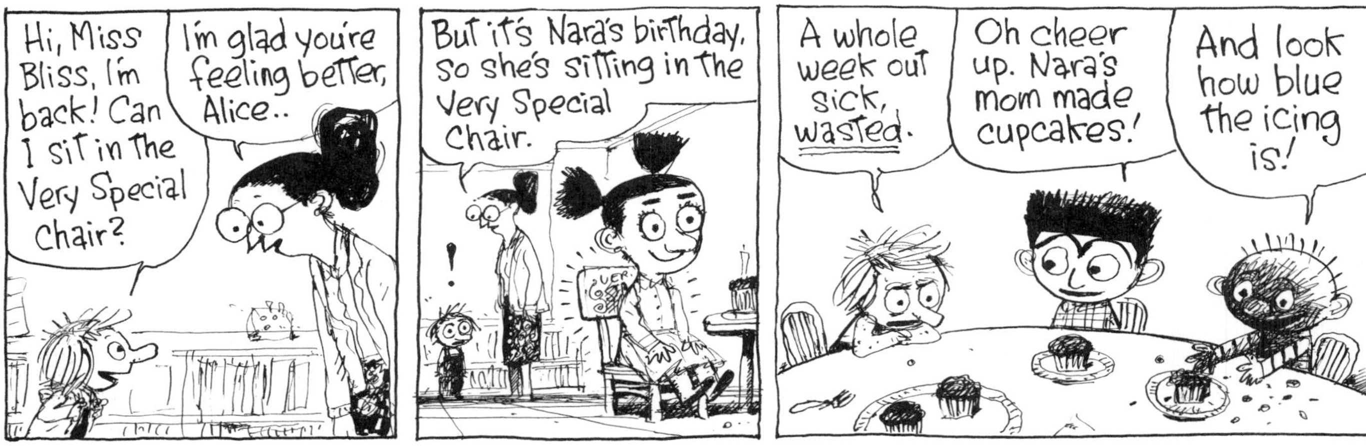
Hi, Miss Bliss, I'm back! Can I sit in the Very Special Chair?
I'm glad you're feeling better, Alice..
But it's Nara's birthday, so she's sitting in the Very Special Chair.
!
A whole week out sick, wasted.
Oh cheer up. Nara's mom made cupcakes!
And look how blue the icing is!

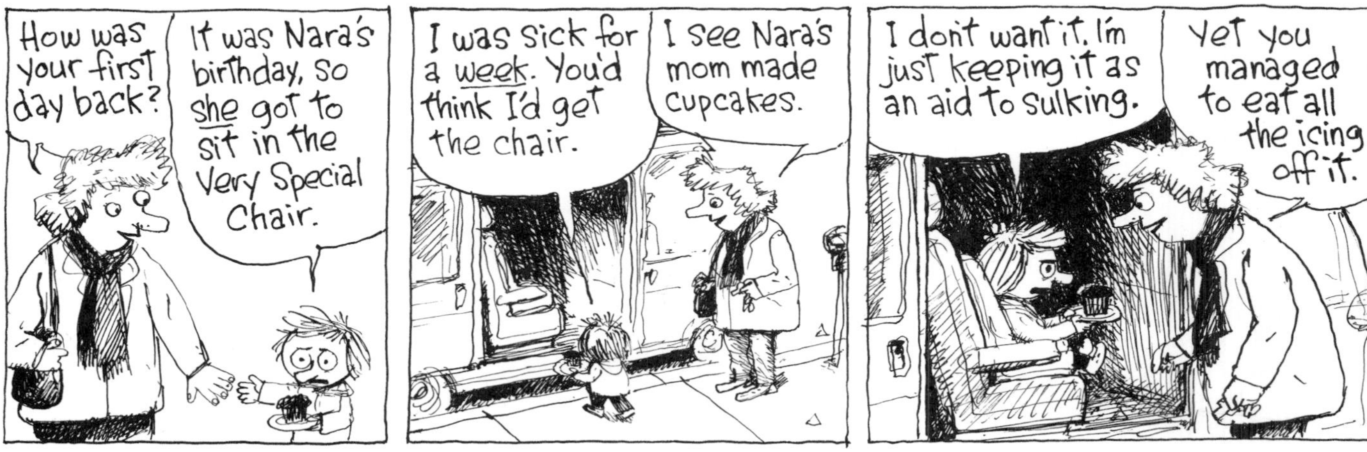
How was your first day back?
It was Nara's birthday, so she got to sit in the Very Special Chair.
I was sick for a week. You'd think I'd get the chair.
I see Nara's mom made cupcakes.
I don't want it. I'm just keeping it as an aid to sulking.
Yet you managed to eat all the icing off it.

This was, as they say, inspired by a true-life incident.

Please note the uninspired, stunted snowmen. These are the types I believe are more often built by small children who lose interest fast and can't be bothered to build the more complex three-part classic snowmen. And forget the carrot nose and coal eyes, or the scarf and top hat. Who can even find that stuff anymore?

Creativity + Neatness = Art isn't too far off, but there are a few things missing. Such as clarity, purpose, surprise, know-how, perspiration, and something to put under it all, such as a newspaper, so the table stays nice.

My daughter did this, and now for hundreds of years people will find little smiley pebbles in our neighborhood and wonder why.

Alice is the strange little kid who stares at you so fixedly in a restaurant or other public place until you're overcome by self-consciousness. Please note the breaking of the fourth wall.

Ew, a sticky floor. Aren't you glad I got the fourth wall fixed in time?

A cheap-shot definition of the oboe is that it's an ill wind that nobody blows well. Me, I love the oboe.

Though I might find an eight year old practicing the oboe every day to be a little trying.

I swiped Mr. Otterloop's little joke from a very old *Mad Magazine*. Shh, don't tell.

Dill, what's that thing in your yard?

My brothers are building a trebuchet.

It's like a catapult. It can throw things real far.

They've promised me a ride in it when it's finished!

LUCKY. Can I come, too?

Dill's brothers' first trebuchet. It's rendered pretty accurately, too, if anybody needs a schematic for building your own.

Dill's brothers are building a trebuchet. Why doesn't Petey build stuff?

Petey made a very nice horse-head bookend for me once.

I keep it up high on the shelf with all my favorite fragile things.

I pinched my finger doing it, too. See the scar?

Big deal! How many horse-head books do we have anyway?

Alice.

Alice, where are you taking that ice cube tray?

Up to the bathroom.

If you flush an ice cube down the potty before you go to bed, it'll snow that night for sure! I'm going to dump the whole tray in!

Or you could go to the store and get some bags of party ice—

You may flush one ice cube, Alice.

This is also drawn from life, and is believed by many to be effective.

Look! What's that?

What?

Oh, it's just a pile of snow.

It's so big.

They call it Old Mount Soot. It forms in the parking lot every year whether it snows or not.

Mom, can I climb on it?

No, it's dirty.

On its icy, begrimed slopes dwell tiny, dirty trolls called the Sooti. They sneak down and carry off unwary bargain-hunting shoppers to their doom.

Really?

That's why you find abandoned shopping carts everywhere.

Wow. Nature is so cool.

Look! Here's a cart, and somebody's left all their coupons in it!

As I might've mentioned, I love the notion that some unremarkable, commonplace thing, such as a pile of dirty snow, might inspire a whole new mythology. At least for Petey.

C'mon, Petey! You can do it!

Mom, I don't know—

GO, PETEY, GO!

NO, WAIT, I CAAAAAAA

Omigosh— Petey?

MUSH

PETEY? CAN YOU STAND UP?

I–I don't know—

Yeah, I guess so.

YAY! WHO'S MOM'S BIG BOY? LET'S DO IT AGAIN!

ARE YOU CRAZY? ARE YOU TRYING TO KILL ME?

Is your brother in another awkward stage?

I call it "Keeping Mom's Expectations Low" and I'm all for it.

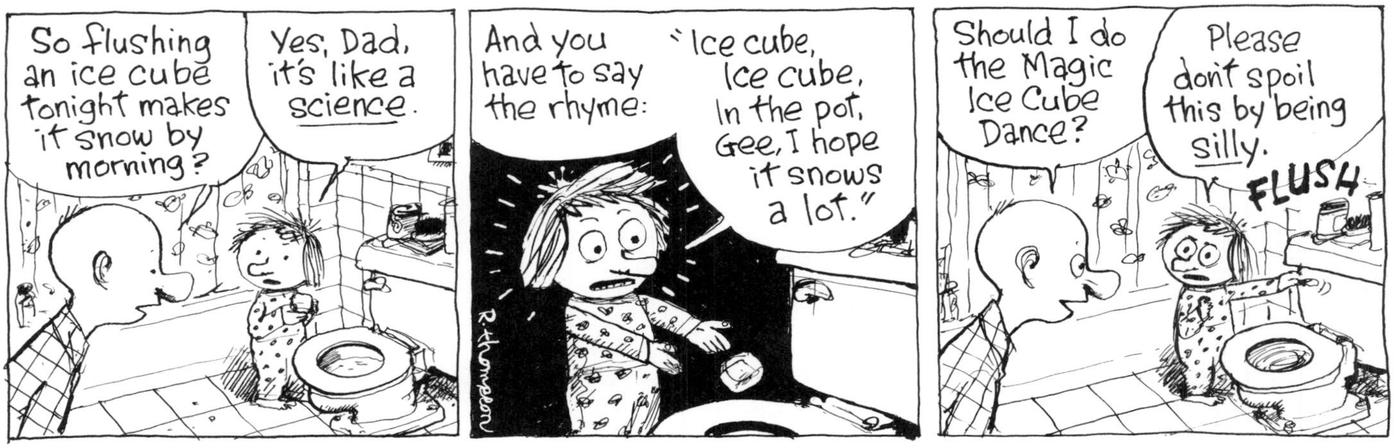
So flushing an ice cube tonight makes it snow by morning?
Yes, Dad, it's like a science.
And you have to say the rhyme:
"Ice cube, Ice cube, In the pot, Gee, I hope it snows a lot."
Should I do the Magic Ice Cube Dance?
Please don't spoil this by being silly.
FLUSH

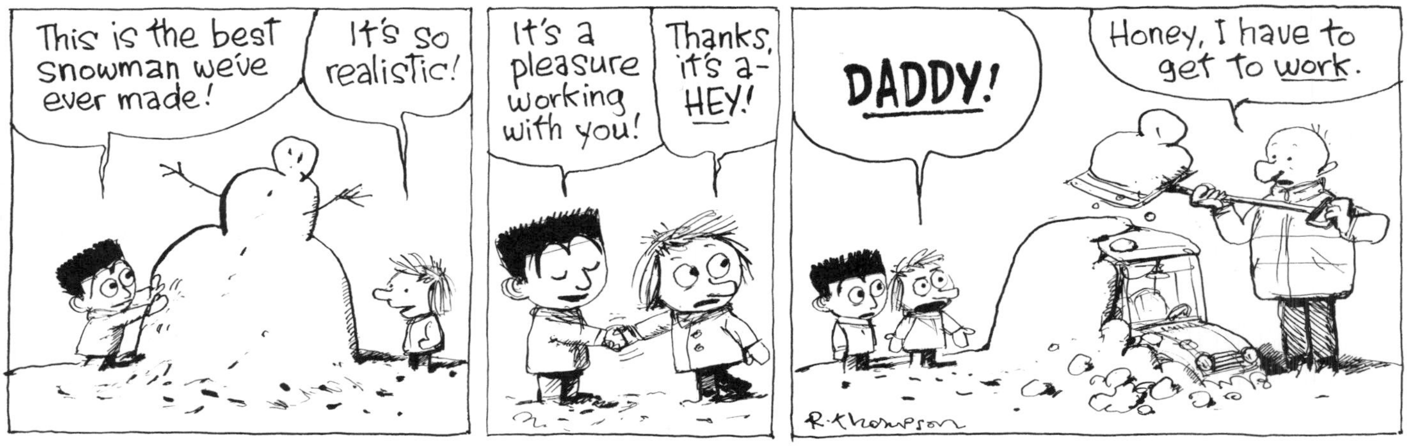
This is the best snowman we've ever made!
It's so realistic!
It's a pleasure working with you!
Thanks, it's a- HEY!
DADDY!
Honey, I have to get to work.

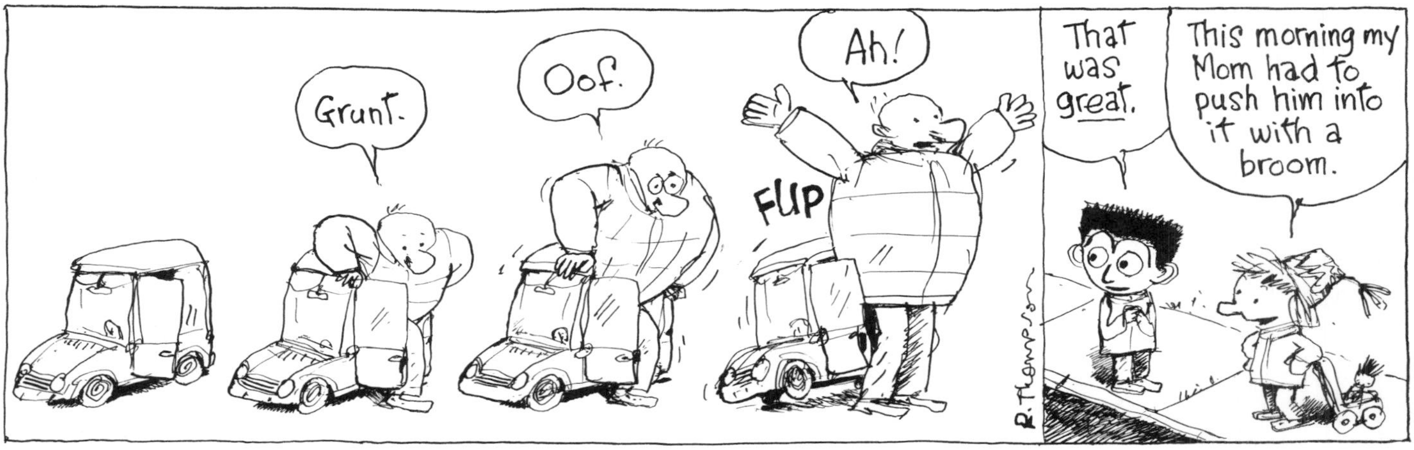
Grunt.
Oof.
FUP
Ah!
That was great.
This morning my Mom had to push him into it with a broom.

Drawing a forced-perspective view such as the one in panel two is very enjoyable. Making it read clearly can be difficult, but it works well for cramming things into a small panel and gives it an interesting, toy-theater feel.

87

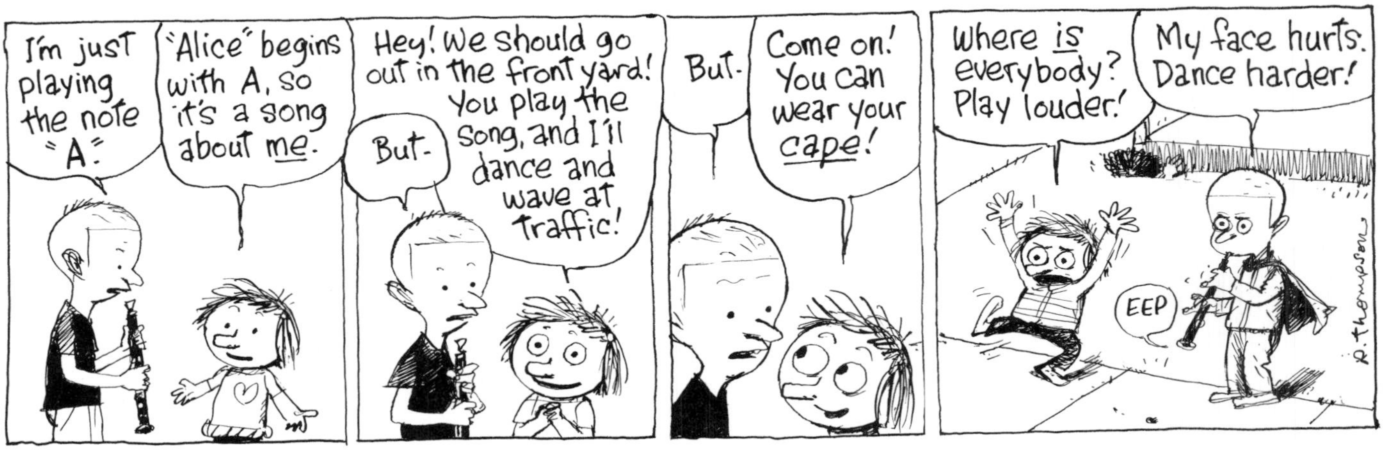
I'm just playing the note "A."
"Alice" begins with A, so it's a song about me.
Hey! We should go out in the front yard! You play the song, and I'll dance and wave at traffic!
But-
But-
Come on! You can wear your cape!
Where is everybody? Play louder!
My face hurts. Dance harder!
EEP

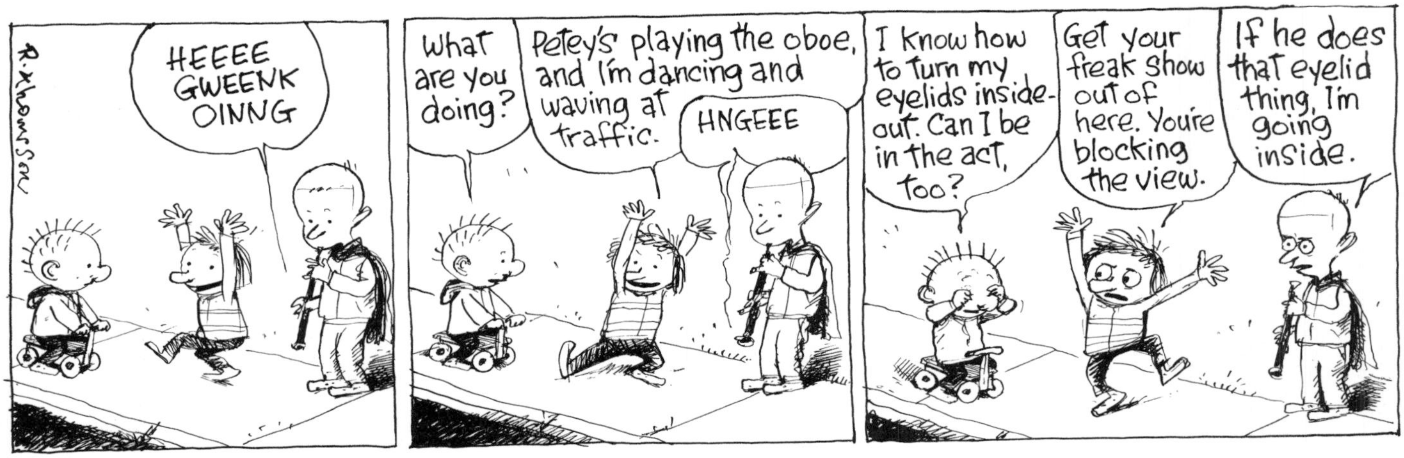
HEEEE GWEENK OINNG
What are you doing?
Petey's playing the oboe, and I'm dancing and waving at traffic.
HNGEEE
I know how to turn my eyelids inside-out. Can I be in the act, too?
Get your freak show out of here. You're blocking the view.
If he does that eyelid thing, I'm going inside.

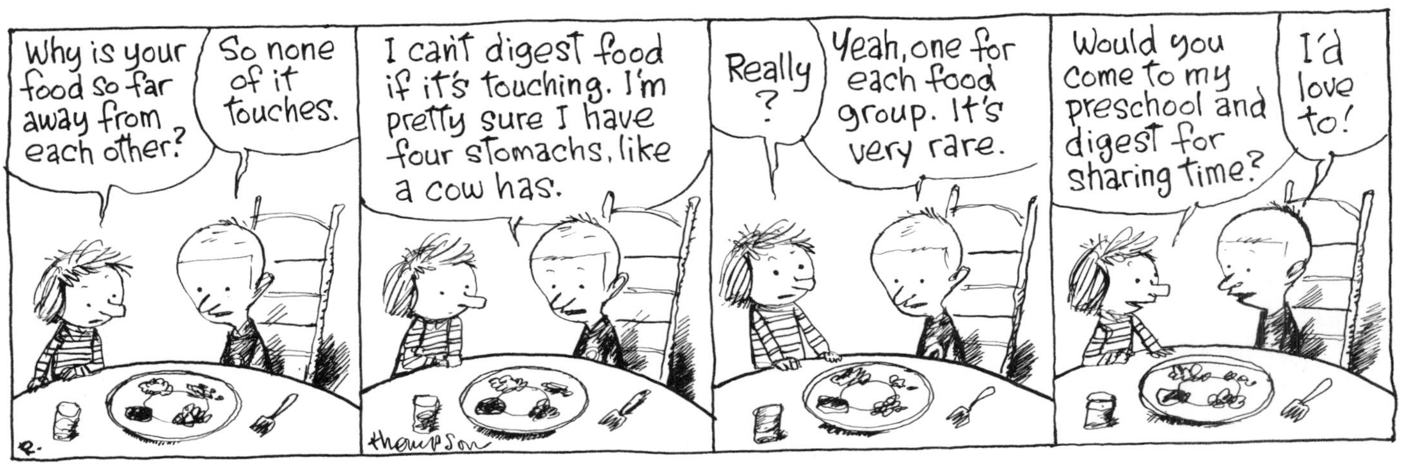
Why is your food so far away from each other?
So none of it touches.
I can't digest food if it's touching. I'm pretty sure I have four stomachs, like a cow has.
Really?
Yeah, one for each food group. It's very rare.
Would you come to my preschool and digest for sharing time?
I'd love to!

Petey elevates his limitations, turning them from character flaws into qualities worth studying and imitating. You'll note the 108-year-old guy gets a bottle of wine with his fungus, so it can't be too bad.

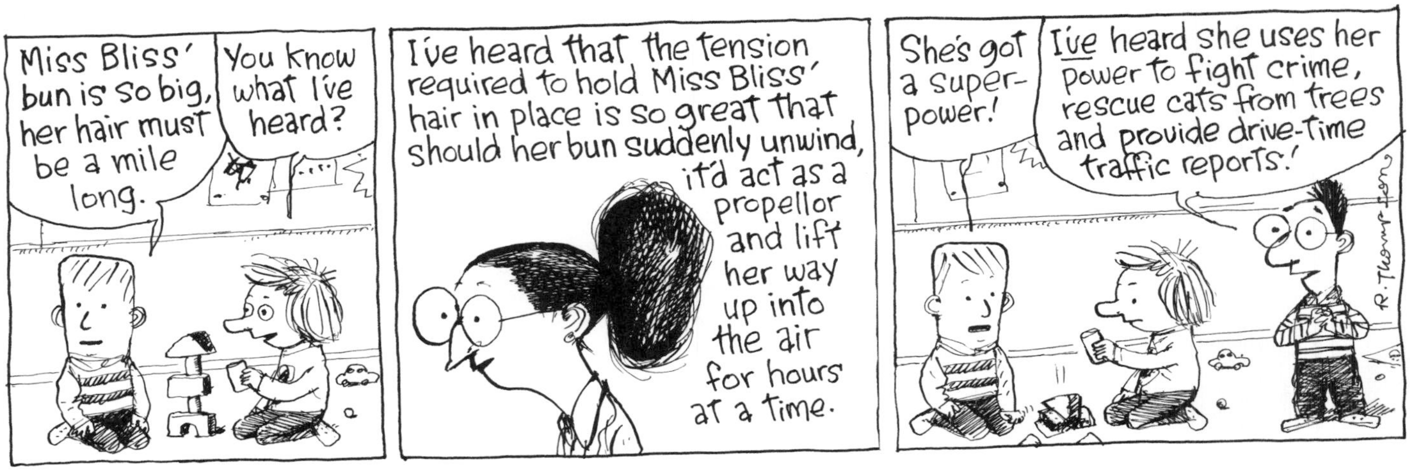
Miss Bliss' bun is so big, her hair must be a mile long.
You know what I've heard?
I've heard that the tension required to hold Miss Bliss' hair in place is so great that should her bun suddenly unwind, it'd act as a propellor and lift her way up into the air for hours at a time.
She's got a super-power!
I've heard she uses her power to fight crime, rescue cats from trees and provide drive-time traffic reports!

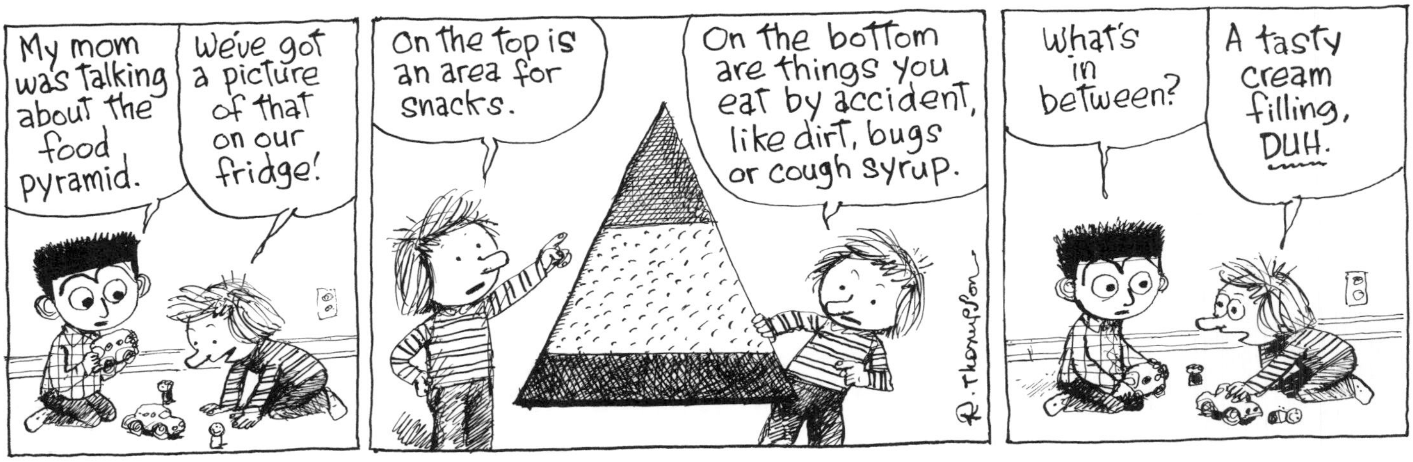
My mom was talking about the food pyramid.
We've got a picture of that on our fridge!
On the top is an area for snacks.
On the bottom are things you eat by accident, like dirt, bugs or cough syrup.
What's in between?
A tasty cream filling, DUH.

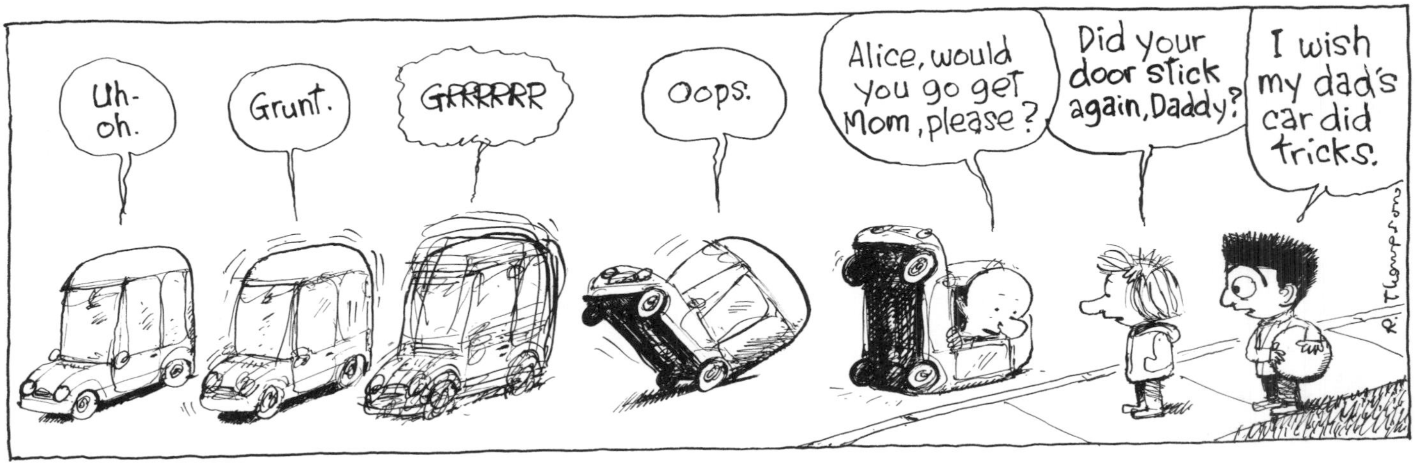
Uh-oh.
Grunt.
GRRRRRR
Oops.
Alice, would you go get Mom, please?
Did your door stick again, Daddy?
I wish my dad's car did tricks.

This has happened to every parent I know, whether they'll admit it or not. I'll bet emergency rooms treat dozens of broken noses every year by a parent too embarrassed to say what really happened.

The first time I noticed the moon out during the day, I was in first grade and I thought something must've gone really wrong. I blame that *Goodnight Moon* book for my confusion.

In the old *Washington Post Magazine* strips, Mrs. Otterloop very briefly worked for a handicraft store that sold crafty things like the juice-box caddy. I dropped that, as it seemed a little stereotypical; she ought to work at something unexpected, like as a crane operator, or as a truck driver, or as a motivational speaker.

"March comes in on clumsy feet, Kicks the trash cans down the street, Spills some garbage on the lawn, Blows the rest to hellandgone, Knocks the branches off the trees, Gives the power lines a squeeze, Then March leaves and as it goes, The sun comes out and then it snows."

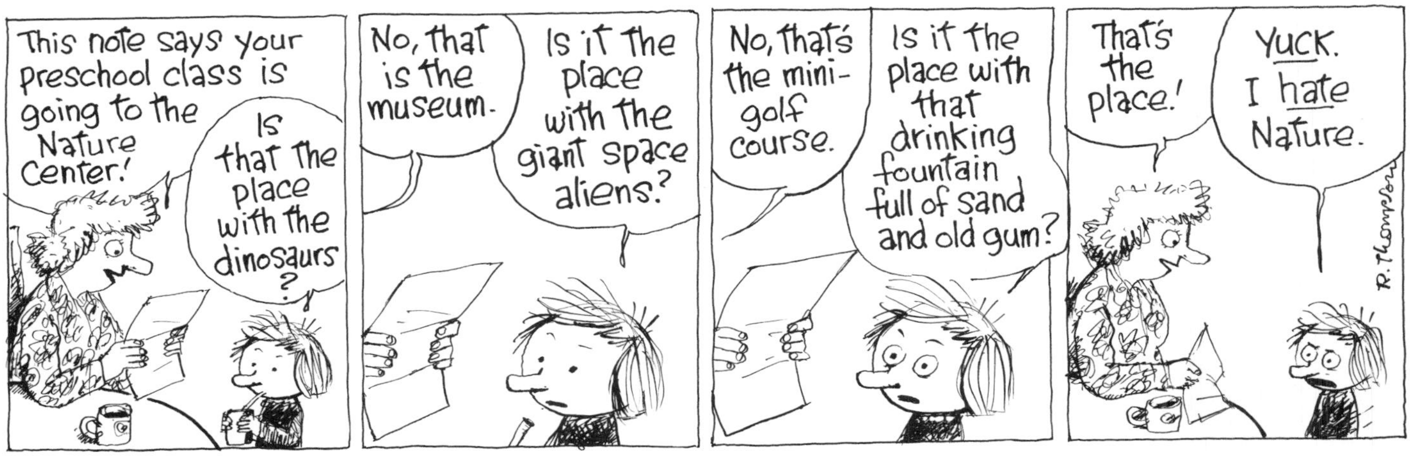
This note says your preschool class is going to the Nature Center!
Is that the place with the dinosaurs?
No, that is the museum.
Is it the place with the giant space aliens?
No, that's the mini-golf course.
Is it the place with that drinking fountain full of sand and old gum?
That's the place!
YUCK. I hate Nature.

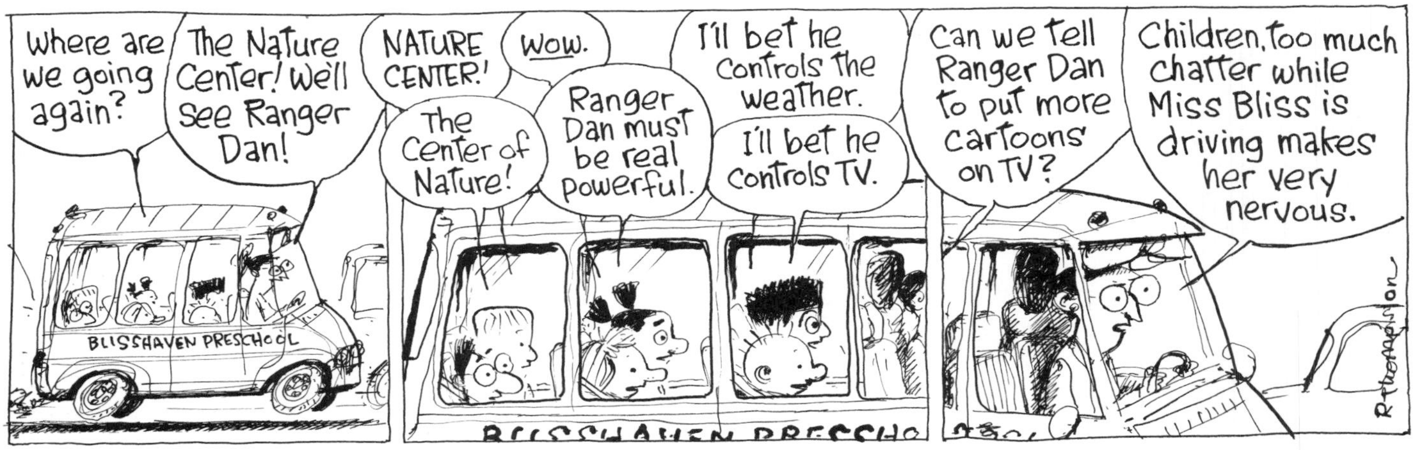
Where are we going again?
The Nature Center! We'll see Ranger Dan!
BLISSHAVEN PRESCHOOL
NATURE CENTER!
WOW.
The Center of Nature!
Ranger Dan must be real powerful.
I'll bet he controls the weather.
I'll bet he controls TV.
Can we tell Ranger Dan to put more cartoons on TV?
Children, too much chatter while Miss Bliss is driving makes her very nervous.

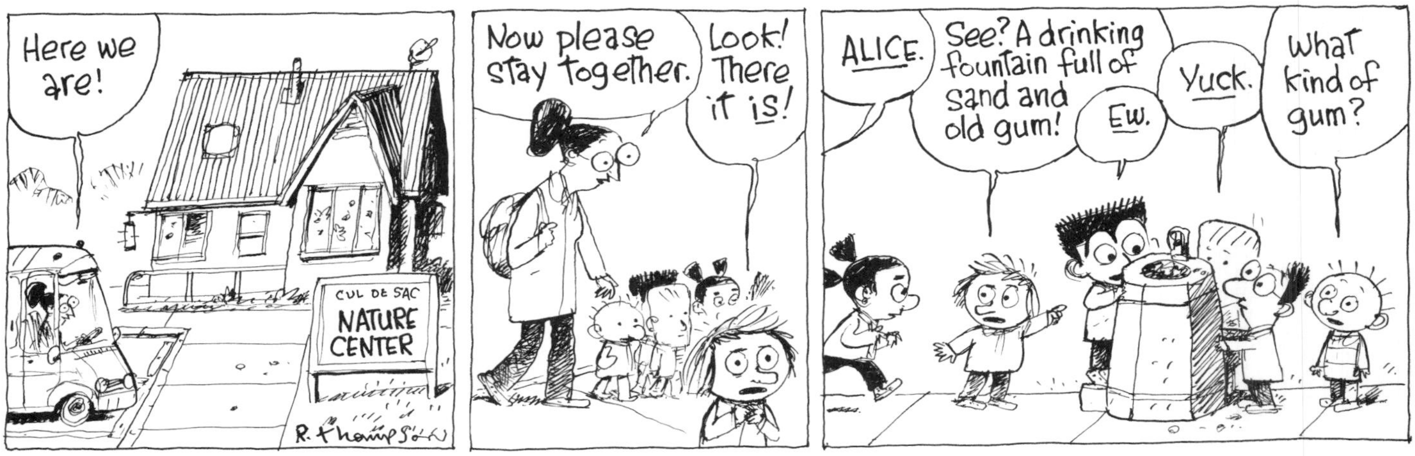
Here we are!
CUL DE SAC
NATURE CENTER
Now please stay together.
Look! There it is!
ALICE.
See? A drinking fountain full of sand and old gum!
Ew.
Yuck.
What kind of gum?

I tried to make Ranger Dan as indoorsy and unranger looking as possible. He's right, though; owls are not all that bright.

And Dill's not the sharpest crayon in the box either.

The job thing Daddy does has not been identified, at least in the syndicated *Cul de Sac*. But it was identified a few times in the *Post* version; Daddy worked at the Department of Consumerism, Office of Petty Complaints, where he was in charge of brochures. Because the strip was set more specifically in Washington, D.C., this all made some sense.

Drawing that intestinal tangle of tube slides is insanely fun.

Dill's brothers again, and I guess there are four, with a wide age range. They'll rarely be shown as they have more power as offstage characters. And if they look anything like Dill, they'd be pretty disappointing in the flesh.

Quackmeyer must've shaken his head instead of nodding it, and Alice got mad at him.

Steering Petey into places outside his very narrow comfort zone is enjoyable and a good way to provoke some minor drama. And it's all for his own good, of course.

98

Where's the trebuchet your brothers built?

It had an accident. They took it out in a field.

They loaded it up and yanked the cord.

And with a mighty TWANG the whole thing fell apart.

No! What did they load it with?

A bag of marshmallows.

What a senseless waste of good food!

BUPF

Will your brothers build another trebuchet?

Not yet. First I want them to build something for me.

I want a giant pinching machine that's able to reach for miles so I can pinch my enemies long distance.

Dill, you don't have any enemies.

Won't you be glad such a device is in good hands?

Dill sometimes shows signs of having a dark side. Because he's the smallest of five poorly socialized and semidiabolical brothers, who can blame him?

So guess what? Miss Bliss is having a contest to name our class!

Uh.

It has to start with a "B."

So we'll be the Blisshaven B-Somethings.

Whoever thinks of the best name gets a prize!

And they get to be Star of the week!

The Blisshaven Brother-Bothering Baloney Brains.

HA! That's way too long!

99

We're having a contest to name our class at Blisshaven. It has to start with the "B" sound, whatever that is.

B goes "BUH."

BUH! Buh! Buh buh. Buh buh buh buh buh buh buh buh buh buh buh buh

buh buh buh. SPOON! The Blisshaven Spoons!

Butter knife!

Bacteria!

PETEY.

My idea for a class name is The Blisshaven Cows.

That doesn't start with B.

My idea will win because everybody loves cows. They provide us with ice cream and cheese and — what did you say?

"Cow" doesn't start with B.

OK. The Blisshaven Big Bad Brown Cows with Beefy Bottoms. How's that?

Better.

I didn't win the class-naming contest.

What's the winning name?

The Blisshaven Blooming Blossoms. Nara thought it up.

That's pretty.

She got a sticker as big as her forehead.

Dill's entry was the Blisshaven Basic Cable Providers!

It was my brother's idea!

They stop naming classes past middle school because, obviously, if it were extended through high school, there'd be classes called the Fledgling Burnouts, the Irritating Overachievers, the Smartmouths, the Potential Wasters, and worse.

Mr. Otterloop does have hair but, like Charlie Brown, it blends in with his head. Unless Charlie Brown is bald, in which case I have to rethink everything.

Petey, who is cripplingly self-conscious, has had a few out-of-body experiences, but this is the first time he's proliferated so exponentially. A few more Peteys and he'll have his own team.

This was rewritten five or six times before my editor and I were satisfied with it. It only became funny when Dill admitted defeat in the face of Alice's blinding logic.

"Pancakes" is also one of those words that's comedy gold. "Waffles" is only comedy silver.

Little Neuro is, of course, a parody of the great fantasy strip *Little Nemo in Slumberland*. It has everything *Little Nemo* had except imagination or narrative drive.

What's not shown makes this strip funny. If Dill were shown catching Petey's shoe, it would be less funny.

Petey's generally unhappy with most of the physical world. The part of it that contains sports equipment must drive him crazy.

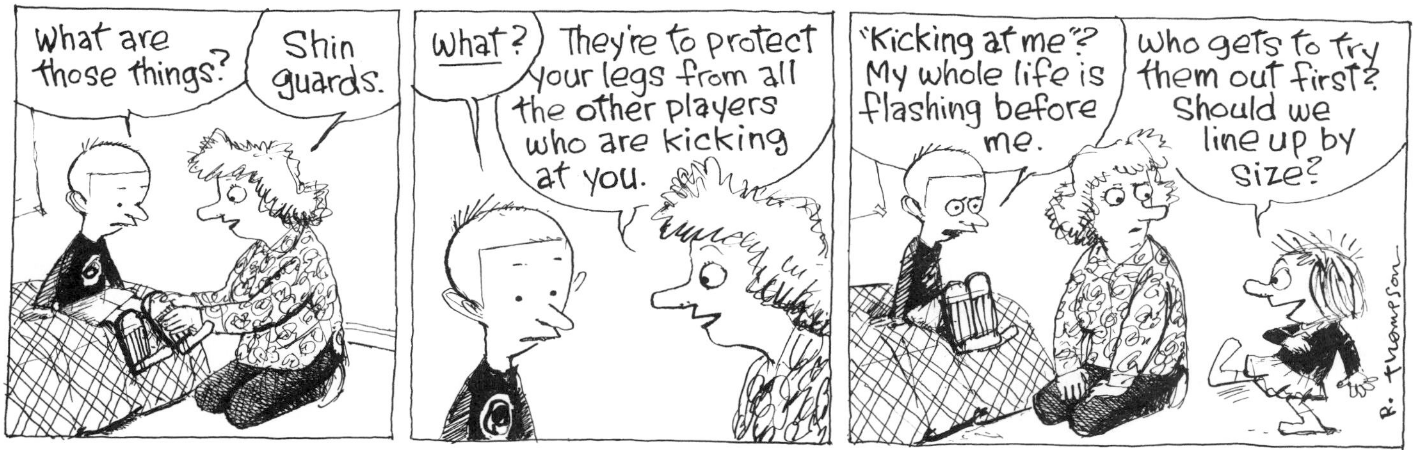
What are those things?
Shin guards.
What?
They're to protect your legs from all the other players who are kicking at you.
"Kicking at me"? My whole life is flashing before me.
Who gets to try them out first? Should we line up by size?
R. Thompson

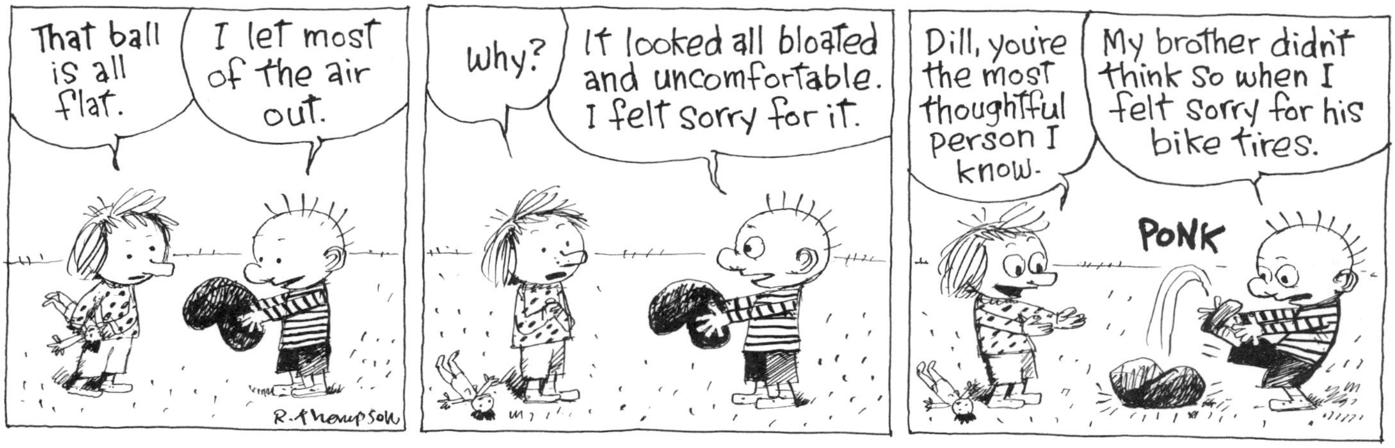
That ball is all flat.
I let most of the air out.
R. Thompson
Why?
It looked all bloated and uncomfortable. I felt sorry for it.
Dill, you're the most thoughtful person I know.
My brother didn't think so when I felt sorry for his bike tires.
PONK

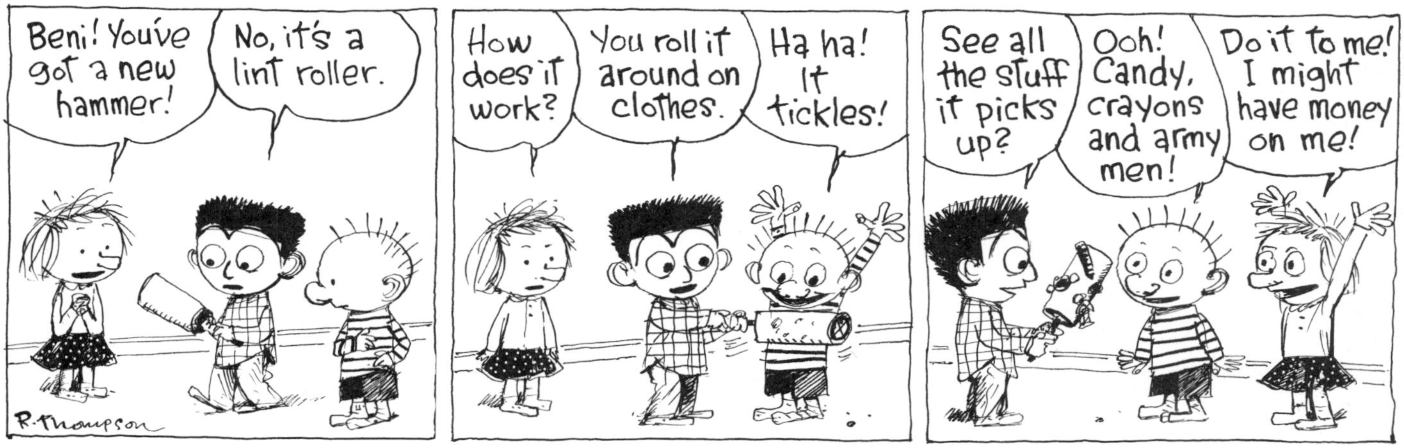
Beni! You've got a new hammer!
No, it's a lint roller.
R. Thompson
How does it work?
You roll it around on clothes.
Ha ha! It tickles!
See all the stuff it picks up?
Ooh! Candy, crayons and army men!
Do it to me! I might have money on me!

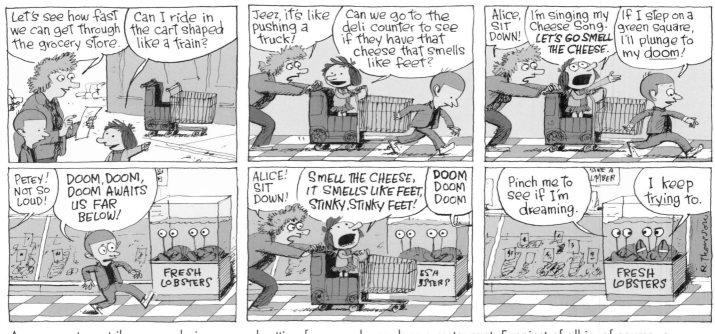

A grocery store strikes me as being a good setting for comedy, as does a restaurant. Funniest of all is, of course, a pancake restaurant.

Toys like this are kind of condescending.

107

I salute you again,

I don't know all of Alice's toys, but in the second panel I recognize Polyfill (extreme right) and Clem Clownpants (in the stripey hat). Clem is later identified not as an actual clown, but as an office worker whose career is stymied by his lousy wardrobe.

Petey has a few totem objects that lend him strength and courage. If he were equipped with all of them, he'd be invincible.

Every preschool classroom has a swaybacked sofa or unsprung chair donated or scrounged by a parent.

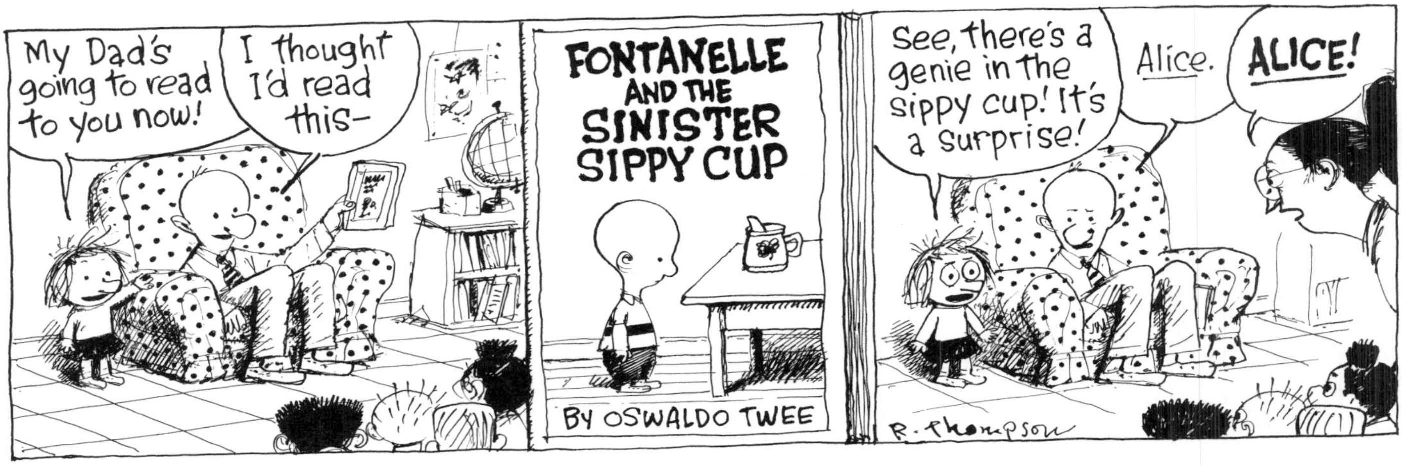
My Dad's going to read to you now!
I thought I'd read this–
FONTANELLE AND THE SINISTER SIPPY CUP
BY OSWALDO TWEE
See, there's a genie in the sippy cup! It's a surprise!
Alice.
ALICE!

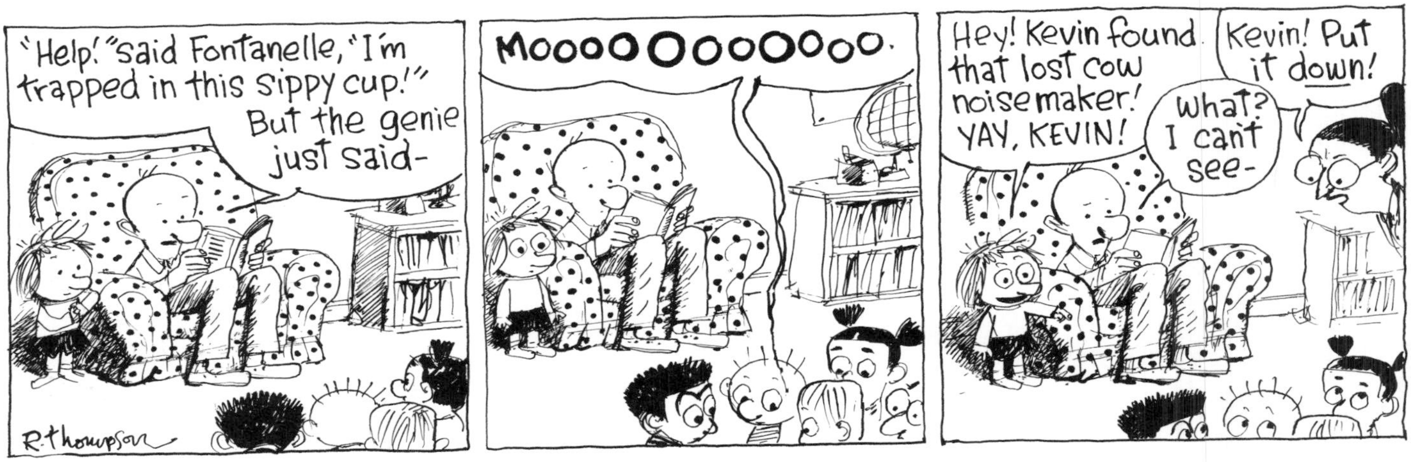
"Help!" said Fontanelle, "I'm trapped in this sippy cup!" But the genie just said–
MOOOOOOOOOOOO.
Hey! Kevin found that lost cow noisemaker! YAY, KEVIN!
Kevin! Put it down!
What? I can't see–

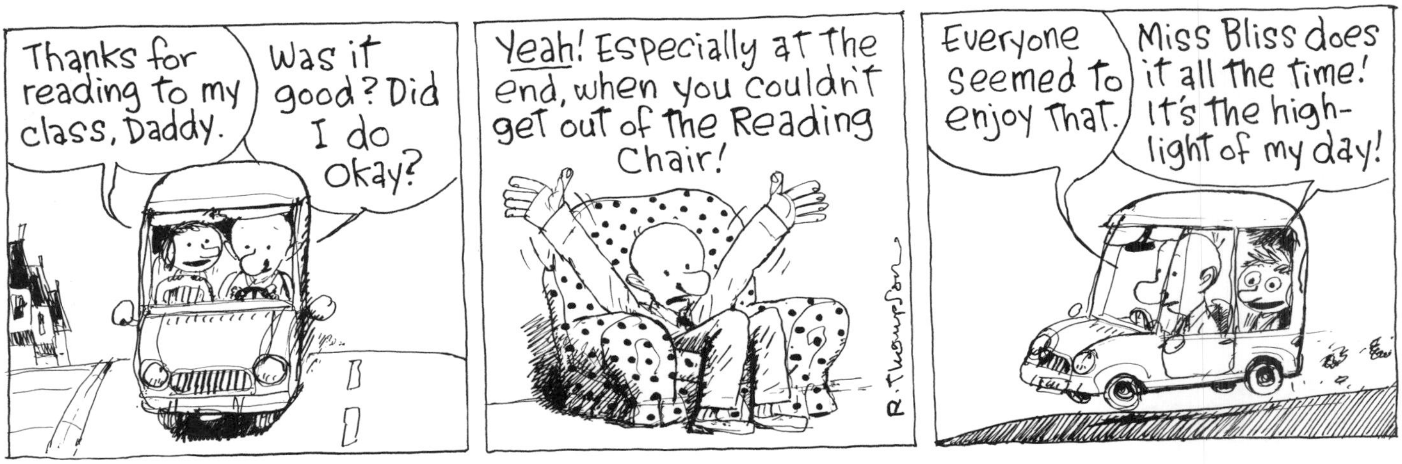
Thanks for reading to my class, Daddy.
Was it good? Did I do okay?
Yeah! Especially at the end, when you couldn't get out of the Reading Chair!
Everyone seemed to enjoy that.
Miss Bliss does it all the time! It's the highlight of my day!

Some show-offy crosshatching in that second panel. Newspaper strips are shrunk to such puny sizes that it's dangerous to crosshatch too much as it reproduces as a fuzzy clot. On the other hand, fuzzy clots are funny.

111

SPRING

POP

THERE HE IS! LET'S GET HIM! NO!

NO! SPORES! POLLEN! GAH!

Petey'd get more respect if he was allergic to bears.

Or chipmunks.

Are we going to talk or are we going to tunnel to Disney World?

If it's this personal, maybe Petey's aversion to nature is well founded.

Is your mom still scrap-booking your stuff?

Now she's saving everything I touch.

Last night I played tic-tac-toe on a children's menu at a pizza restaurant.

Mom took the menu home and put it in a scrapbook along with the napkin I used and a photo of me with the waiter.

My dad read her a magazine article about how parents today have fallen victim to the cult of the child.

About how they've fetishized their kids and worship them as miniature deities.

And yet no one will push me on this stupid swing.

Mom glued the article into a scrap-book. I feel like I'm being stalked by a deranged fan.

Note Alice's fashion doll, which never seems to be wearing clothes. I think it's vain and demanding, and Alice gets fed up with it.

The Otterloops are shown at mealtimes pretty often, but whatever it is they're eating usually looks pretty unappetizing. I gave up on trying to draw food accurately years ago, except for hamburgers.

OK, and maybe pancakes. But they're comedy gold (see page 102).

Just identifying an echidna, much less the color ecru, suggests Beni's pretty advanced for his age.

The shrub is related to Charlie Brown's kite-eating tree, but it's more omnivorous.

I'd thought of the Sofa Centaur about twenty years ago but I didn't know what to do with it. What it needed was a framing device and a snoring grandma.

That ice-cream store is drawn from one three blocks from my house, and they do serve ice cream that color, mostly to kids Alice's age.

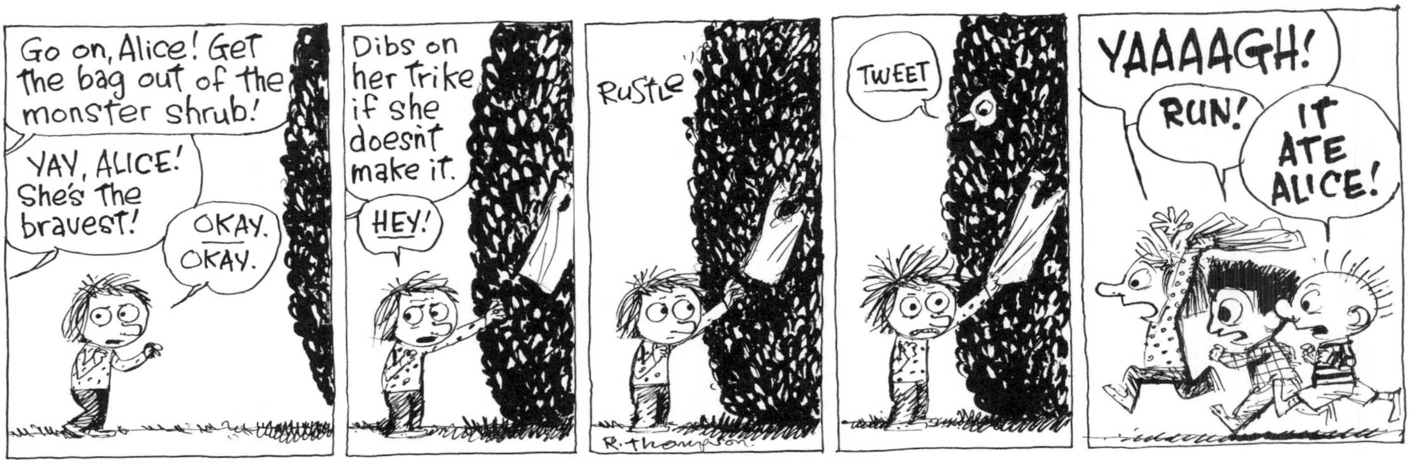
Go on, Alice! Get the bag out of the monster shrub!
YAY, ALICE! She's the bravest!
OKAY. OKAY.
Dibs on her trike if she doesn't make it.
HEY!
RUSTLE
TWEET
YAAAAGH!
RUN!
IT ATE ALICE!

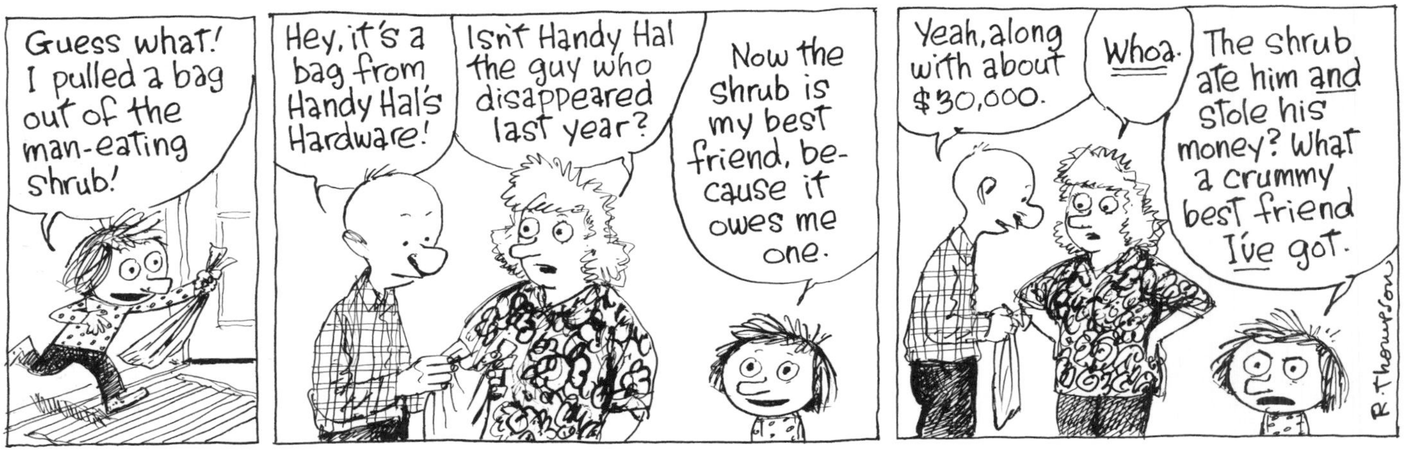
Guess what! I pulled a bag out of the man-eating shrub!
Hey, it's a bag from Handy Hal's Hardware!
Isn't Handy Hal the guy who disappeared last year?
Now the shrub is my best friend, because it owes me one.
Yeah, along with about $30,000.
Whoa.
The shrub ate him and stole his money? What a crummy best friend I've got.

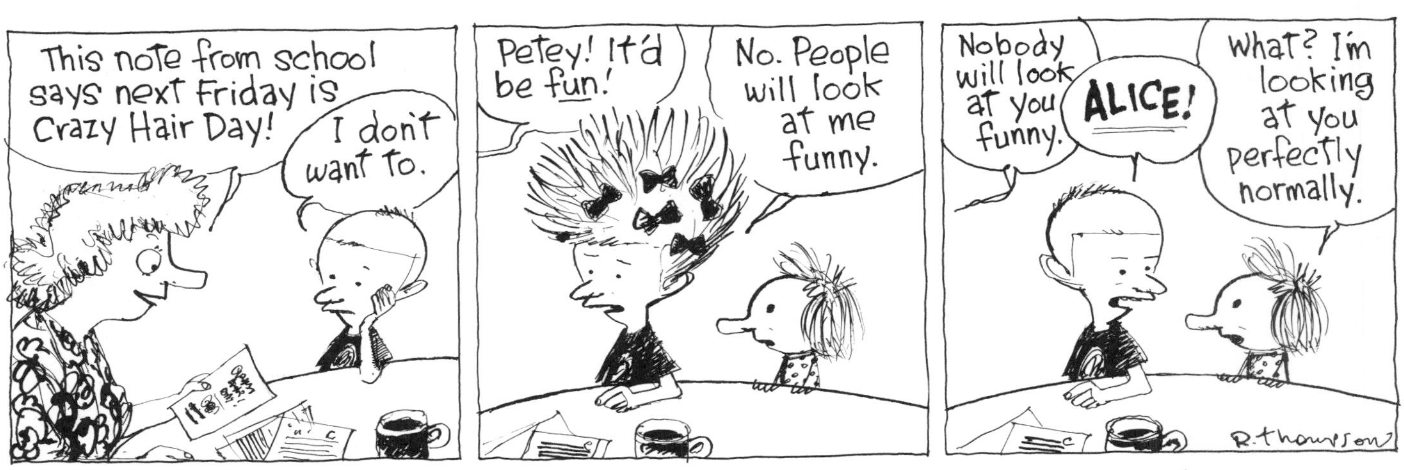
This note from school says next Friday is Crazy Hair Day!
I don't want to.
Petey! It'd be fun!
No. People will look at me funny.
Nobody will look at you funny.
ALICE!
What? I'm looking at you perfectly normally.

Around here schools have Crazy Hair and Pajamas Day, something I was not afflicted with in my academic career.

Alice's taunt in the second panel is inspired by a bit cut out of *The Adventures of Huckleberry Finn*. Two brawny river-boatmen, preparing to fight, circle each other bragging of their awful prowess and superhuman strength. They never get around to actually fighting though.

Patterns in a black-and-white drawing can be used like colors to give it clarity and liveliness. Or they can just be confusing.

Thus begins the epic adventure of Petey's oboe recital.

When I was Petey's age, I took bagpipe lessons.

Bagpipes, like oboes, are double-reed instruments and vehicles for cheap comedy. Bagpipes, however, are more aggressive than oboes.

121

Though this isn't much alluded to, Mrs. Otterloop's first name is Madeline. Mr. Otterloop's name is Peter, making Petey a junior, which is one more thing for him to worry about.

Again, Dill shows a bit of his dark side. Or maybe it's just his slightly creepy side.

The school motto, "A little learning," is from the first line of a poem by Alexander Pope. The line finishes "is a dangerous thing."

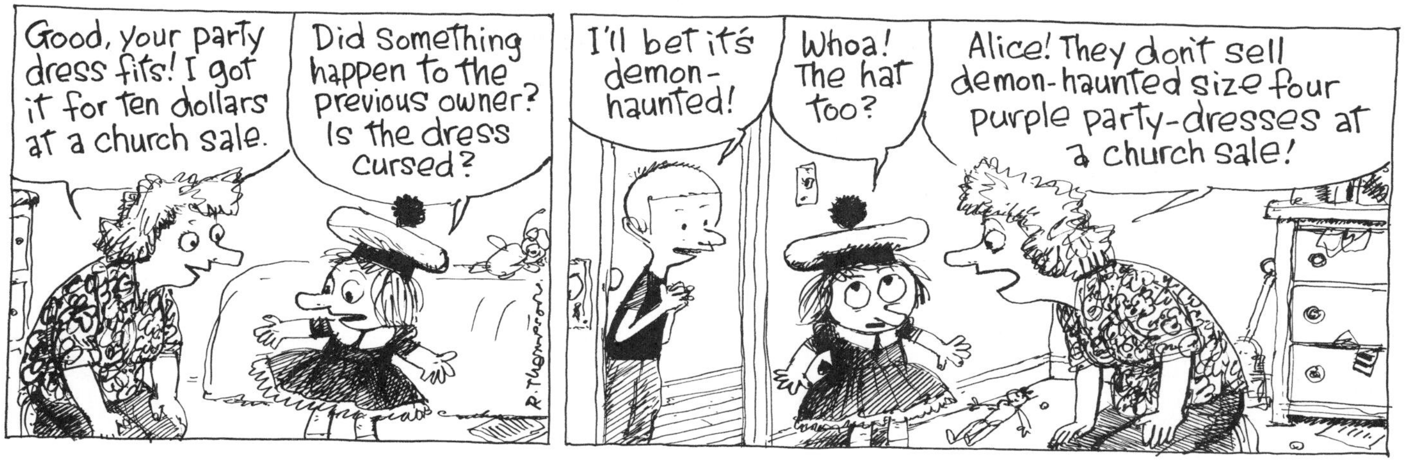
Good, your party dress fits! I got it for ten dollars at a church sale.
Did something happen to the previous owner? Is the dress cursed?
I'll bet it's demon-haunted!
Whoa! The hat too?
Alice! They don't sell demon-haunted size four purple party-dresses at a church sale!
R. Thompson

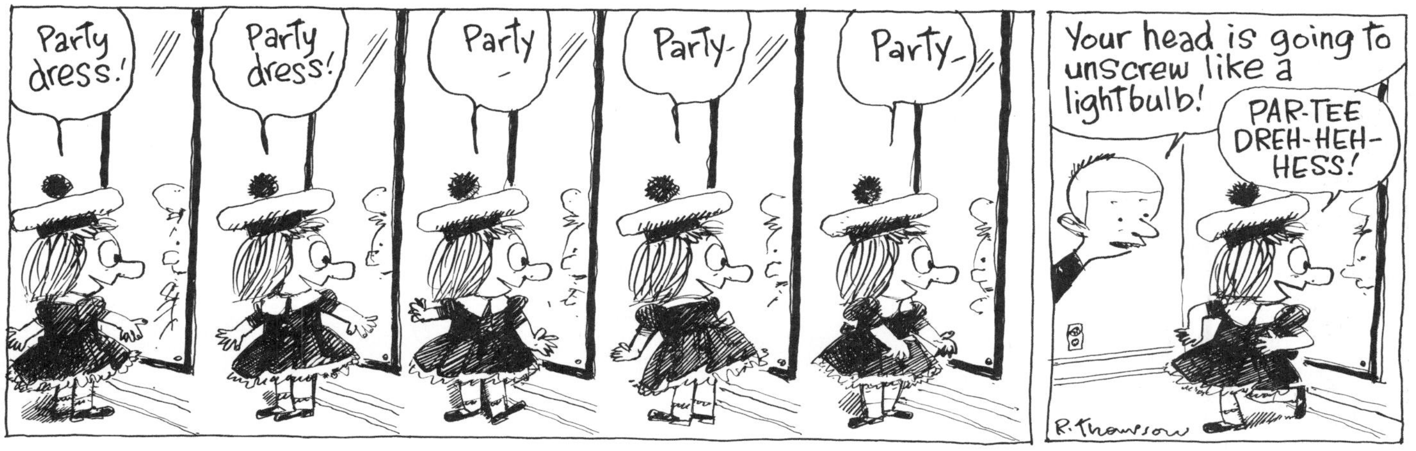
Party dress!
Party dress!
Party
Party-
Party-
Your head is going to unscrew like a lightbulb!
PAR-TEE DREH-HEH-HESS!
R. Thompson

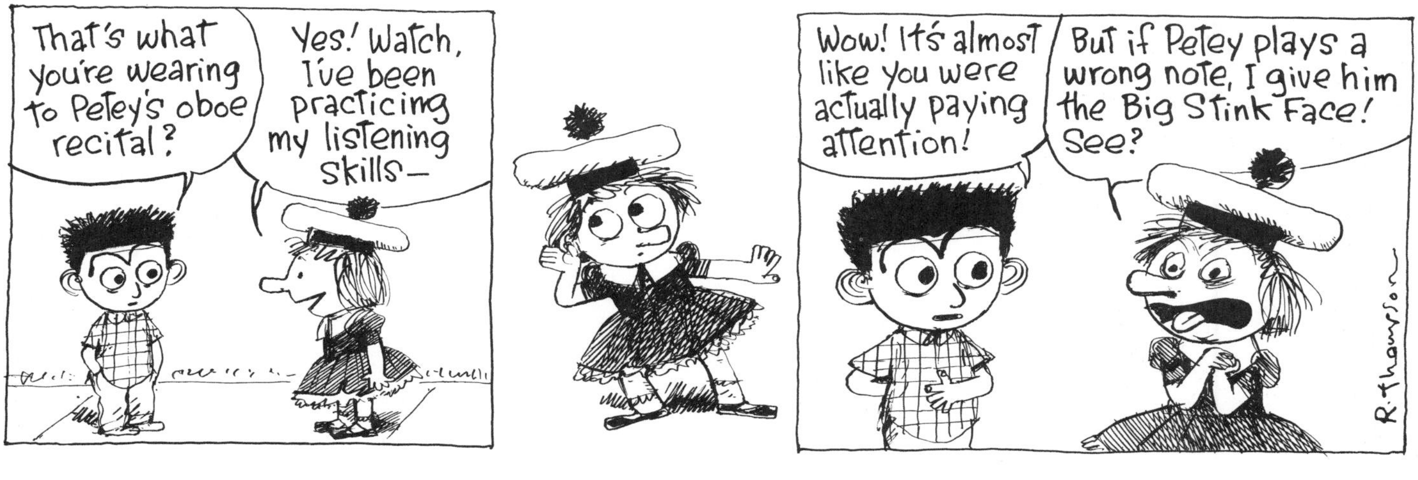
That's what you're wearing to Petey's oboe recital?
Yes! Watch, I've been practicing my listening skills—
Wow! It's almost like you were actually paying attention!
But if Petey plays a wrong note, I give him the Big Stink Face! See?
R. Thompson

Look! There's a bird in the grocery store!

They get in here by accident. There's a whole flock of them.

Every spring they migrate from Fresh Produce to Frozen Foods, and in the fall they go back to Fresh Produce again.

Oh!

And there's an angry herd of stray feral cows that stampedes down the Dairy Aisle every day.

Can we go watch them?

And the lobsters sometimes escape from their tank and rampage around the parking lot.

I hate Rhythm Clapping Game Time.

I need to work on my clapping skills for Petey's recital.

You should bang pot lids together.

My brother banged pot lids together last New Year's Eve and a policeman came and yelled at him, it was so loud.

I don't want the police involved. It'd scare Petey.

I keep missing.

Then don't try fireworks! That New Year's, six policemen came. And a fire truck.

Wow. That's a really bright green.

It's the tie I bought Petey to wear at his recital.

I could just lend him a tie.

One of yours? It'd look like he was wearing a floor-length lobster bib.

He'll have to play real loud to drown out that tie.

It'll be fine. Look, Petey! Here's your new tie!

OW! It's so GREEN!

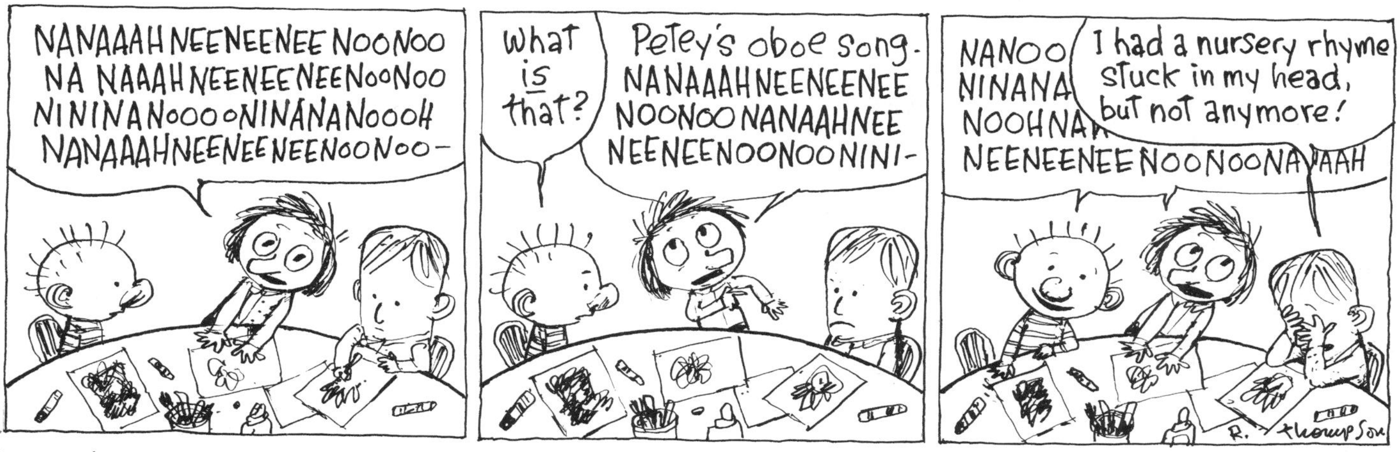
NANAAAH NEENEENEE NOONOO NA NAAAH NEENEENEENOONOO NININANOOOONINANANOOOH NANAAAHNEENEENEENOONOO-
What is that?
Petey's oboe song. NANAAAHNEENEENEE NOONOO NANAAHNEE NEENEENOONOONINI-
NANOO NINANA NOOHNA NEENEENEE NOONOONAAAH
I had a nursery rhyme stuck in my head, but not anymore!

It *is* catchy.

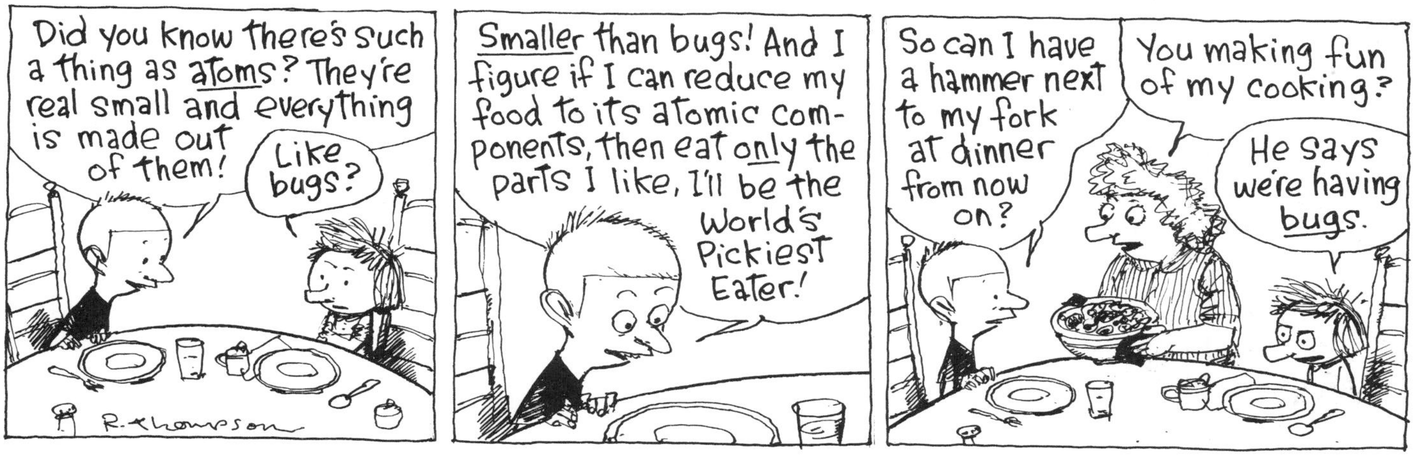
Did you know there's such a thing as atoms? They're real small and everything is made out of them!
Like bugs?
Smaller than bugs! And I figure if I can reduce my food to its atomic components, then eat only the parts I like, I'll be the World's Pickiest Eater!
So can I have a hammer next to my fork at dinner from now on?
You making fun of my cooking?
He says we're having bugs.

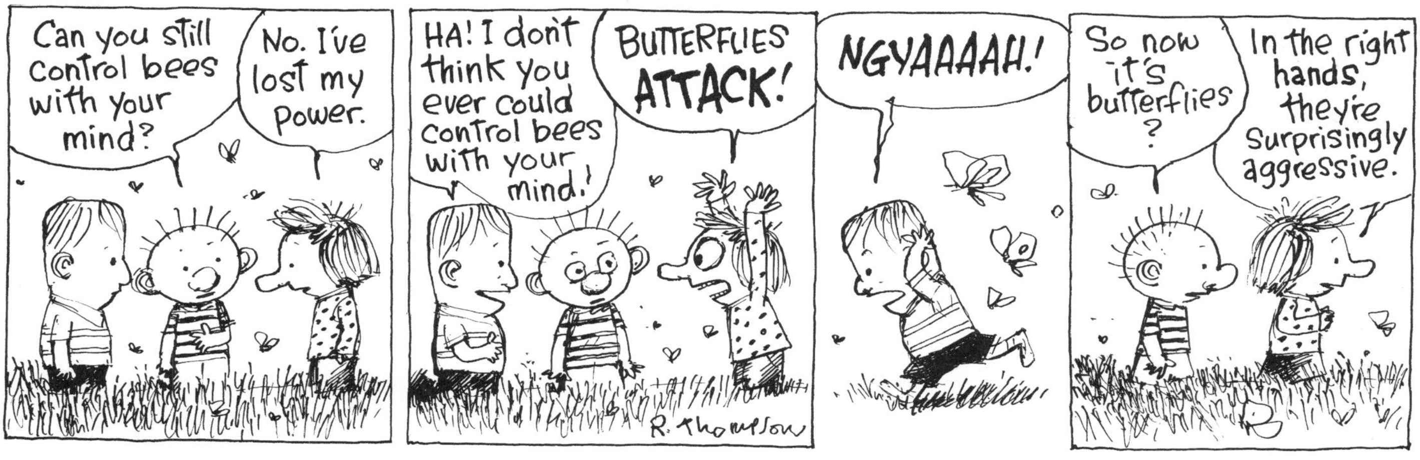
Can you still control bees with your mind?
No. I've lost my power.
HA! I don't think you ever could control bees with your mind!
BUTTERFLIES ATTACK!
NGYAAAAH!
So now it's butterflies?
In the right hands, they're surprisingly aggressive.

I try not to show Mr. Otterloop as a standard-issue Dumped-On Dad, but it's difficult not to sometimes.

It's not suggested that the deviled eggs are meant to be thrown during the performances (see page 34), but it's hard not to jump to that conclusion.

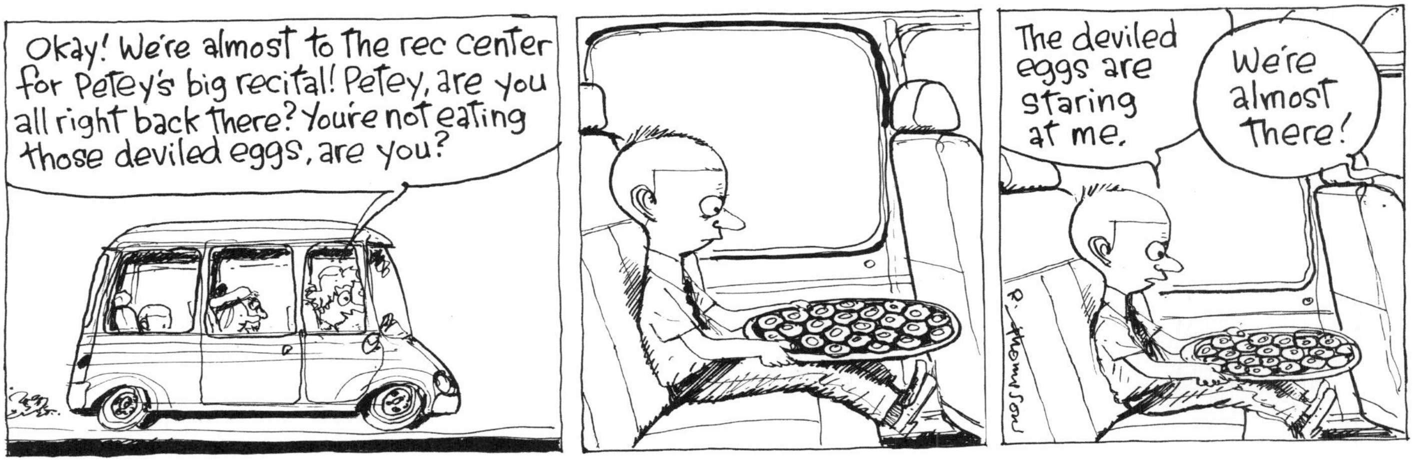
Okay! We're almost to the rec center for Petey's big recital! Petey, are you all right back there? You're not eating those deviled eggs, are you?
The deviled eggs are staring at me.
We're almost there!

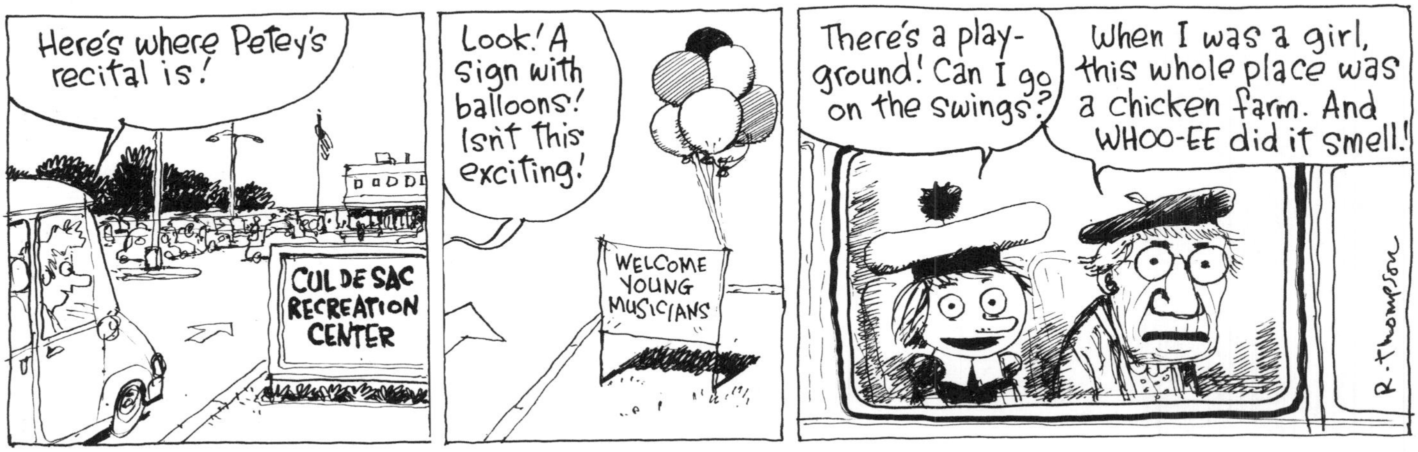
Here's where Petey's recital is!
CUL DE SAC RECREATION CENTER
Look! A sign with balloons! Isn't this exciting!
WELCOME YOUNG MUSICIANS
There's a play-ground! Can I go on the swings?
When I was a girl, this whole place was a chicken farm. And WHOO-EE did it smell!
R. Thompson

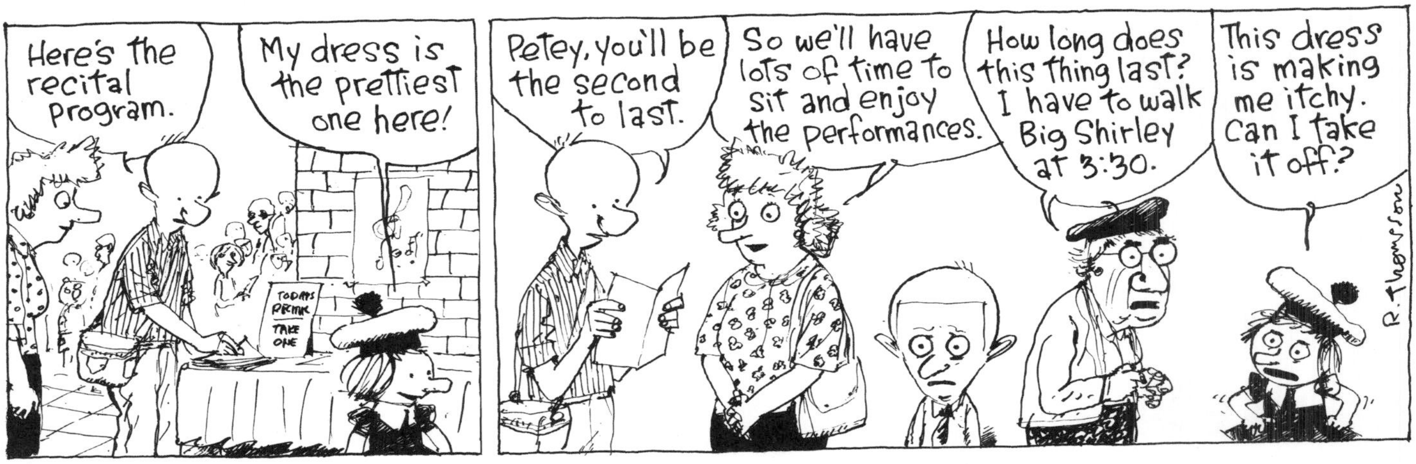
Here's the recital program.
My dress is the prettiest one here!
Petey, you'll be the second to last.
So we'll have lots of time to sit and enjoy the performances.
How long does this thing last? I have to walk Big Shirley at 3:30.
This dress is making me itchy. Can I take it off?
R. Thompson

Mrs. Otterloop's comment about Petey not needing glasses makes me happy.

A crowd scene. Nobody likes drawing crowd scenes, least of all me.

Ernesto Lacuna's second appearance (see page 66).

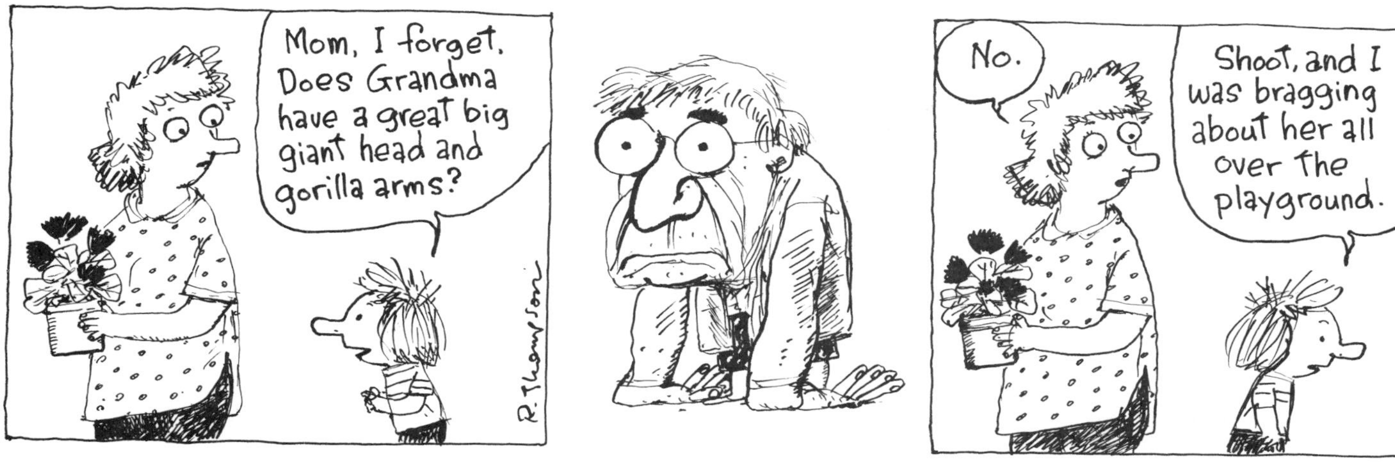
Mom, I forget. Does Grandma have a great big giant head and gorilla arms?
R. Thompson
No.
Shoot, and I was bragging about her all over the playground.

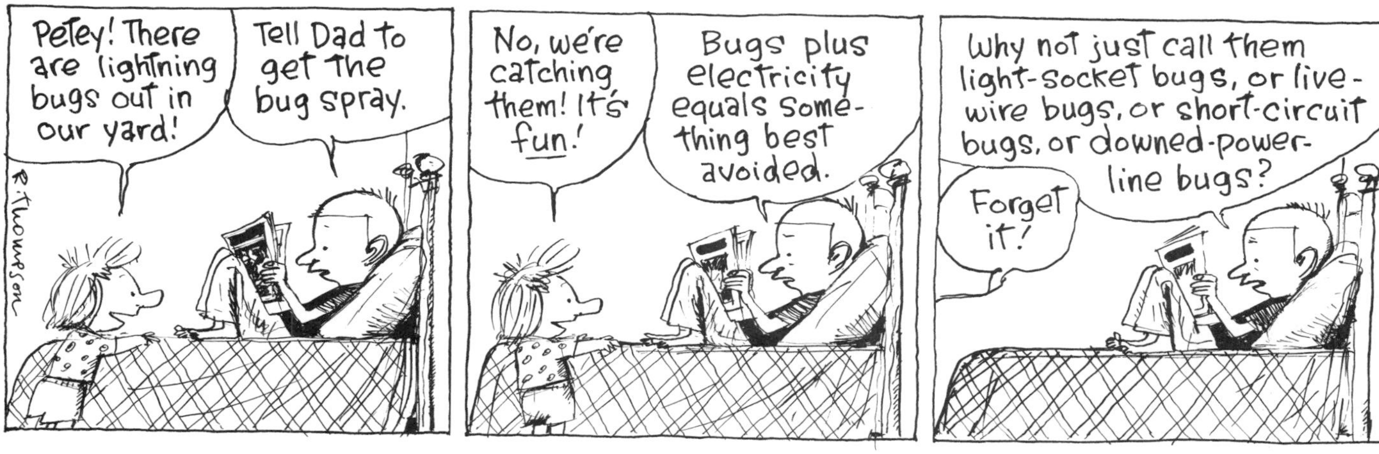
Petey! There are lightning bugs out in our yard!
Tell Dad to get the bug spray.
R. Thompson
No, we're catching them! It's fun!
Bugs plus electricity equals something best avoided.
Why not just call them light-socket bugs, or live-wire bugs, or short-circuit bugs, or downed-power-line bugs?
Forget it!

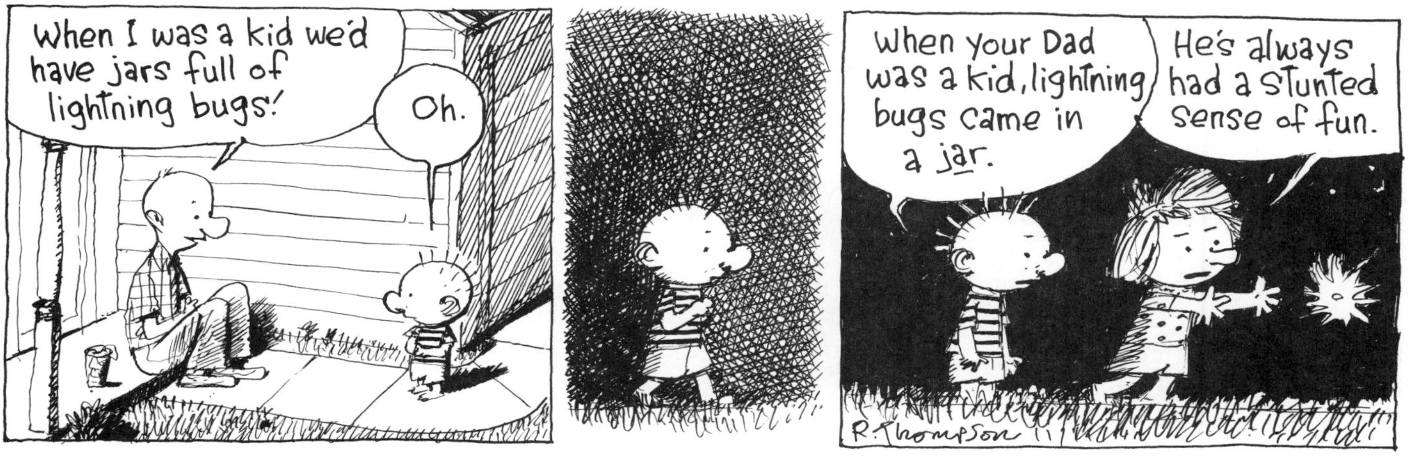
When I was a kid we'd have jars full of lightning bugs!
Oh.
When your Dad was a kid, lightning bugs came in a jar.
He's always had a stunted sense of fun.
R. Thompson

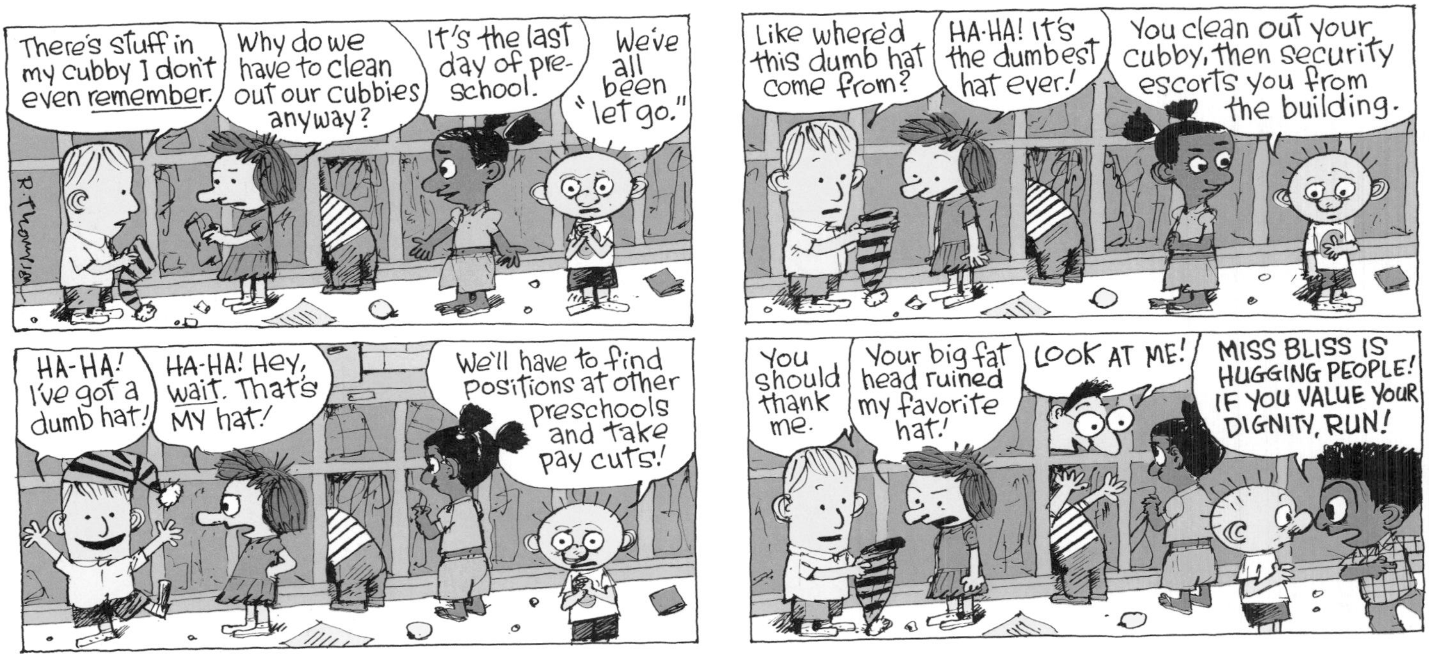
There's stuff in my cubby I don't even remember.
Why do we have to clean out our cubbies anyway?
It's the last day of pre-school.
We've all been "let go."
Like where'd this dumb hat come from?
HA-HA! It's the dumbest hat ever!
You clean out your cubby, then security escorts you from the building.
HA-HA! I've got a dumb hat!
HA-HA! Hey, wait. That's MY hat!
We'll have to find positions at other preschools and take pay cuts!
You should thank me.
Your big fat head ruined my favorite hat!
LOOK AT ME!
MISS BLISS IS HUGGING PEOPLE! IF YOU VALUE YOUR DIGNITY, RUN!

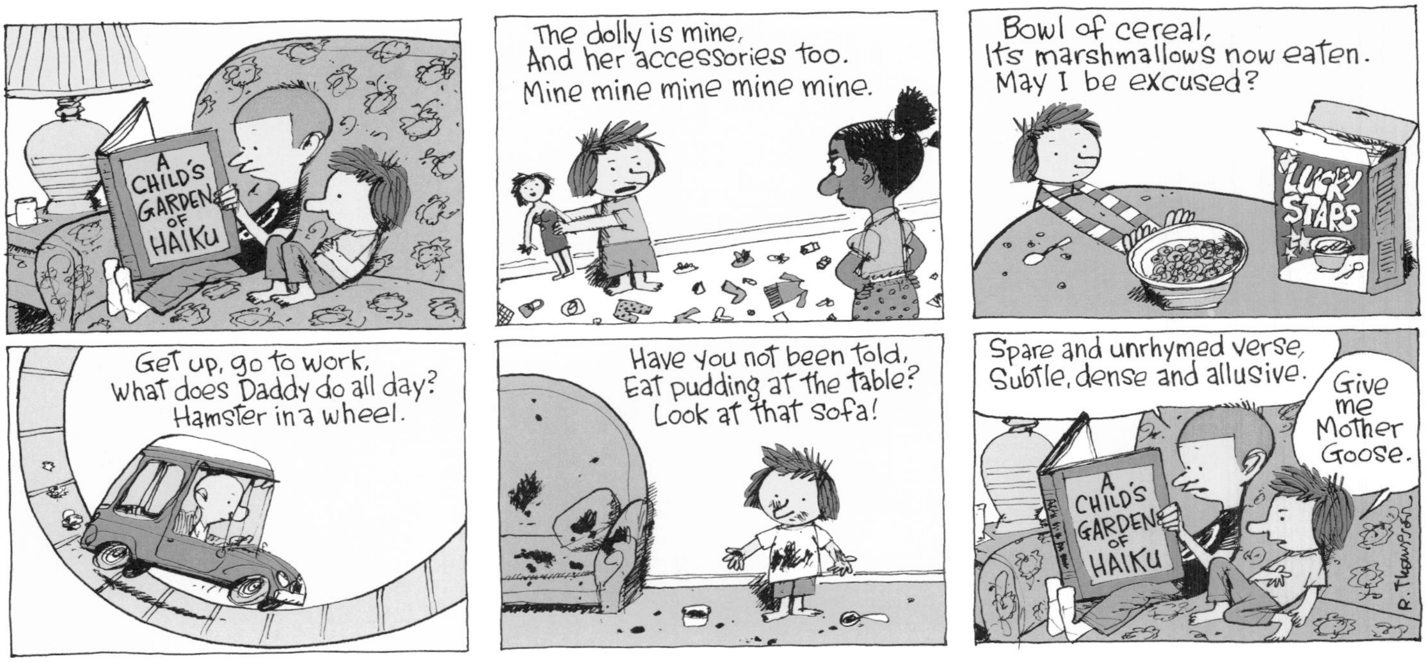
A CHILD'S GARDEN OF HAIKU
The dolly is mine,
And her accessories too.
Mine mine mine mine mine.
Bowl of cereal,
Its marshmallows now eaten.
May I be excused?
LUCKY STARS
Get up, go to work,
What does Daddy do all day?
Hamster in a wheel.
Have you not been told,
Eat pudding at the table?
Look at that sofa!
Spare and unrhymed verse,
Subtle, dense and allusive.
Give me Mother Goose.
A CHILD'S GARDEN OF HAIKU

Medieval engines of war fit in with bland suburban neighborhoods remarkably well.

Petey is likely also a fan of the more somber and intense modern graphic novelists.

Alice, on the other hand, has a deep yet inchoate desire to ride on a float and wave at people.

Please note the stilt-walking Uncle Sam, which is required by law in all Fourth of July parades.

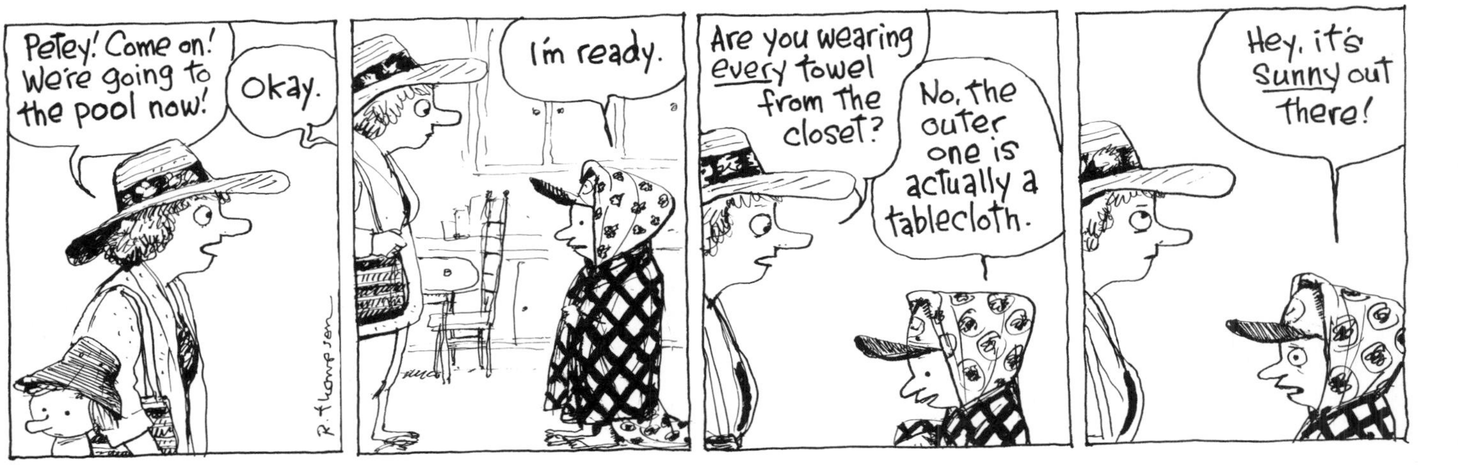
Petey! Come on! We're going to the pool now!
Okay.
R. Thompson
I'm ready.
Are you wearing every towel from the closet?
No, the outer one is actually a tablecloth.
Hey, it's sunny out there!

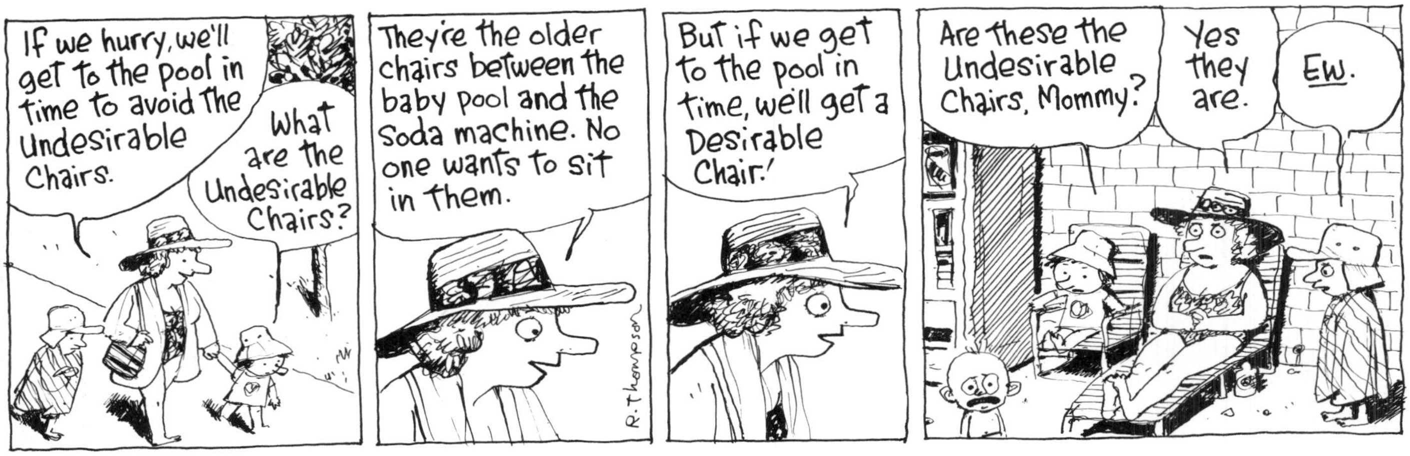
If we hurry, we'll get to the pool in time to avoid the Undesirable Chairs.
What are the Undesirable Chairs?
They're the older chairs between the baby pool and the soda machine. No one wants to sit in them.
R. Thompson
But if we get to the pool in time, we'll get a Desirable Chair!
Are these the Undesirable Chairs, Mommy?
Yes they are.
Ew.

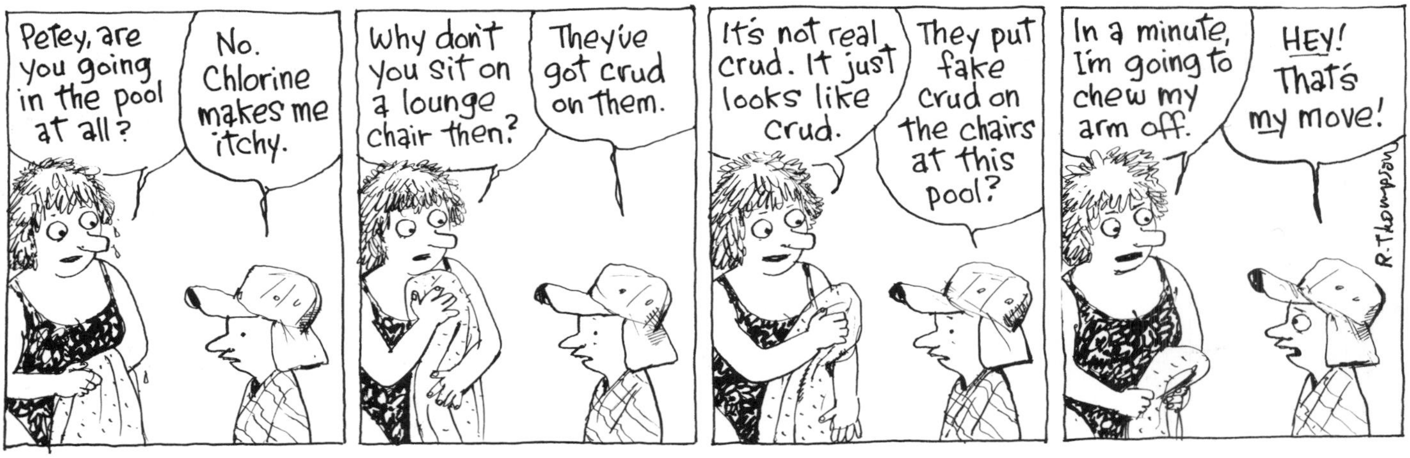
Petey, are you going in the pool at all?
No. Chlorine makes me itchy.
Why don't you sit on a lounge chair then?
They've got crud on them.
It's not real crud. It just looks like crud.
They put fake crud on the chairs at this pool?
In a minute, I'm going to chew my arm off.
HEY! That's my move!
R. Thompson

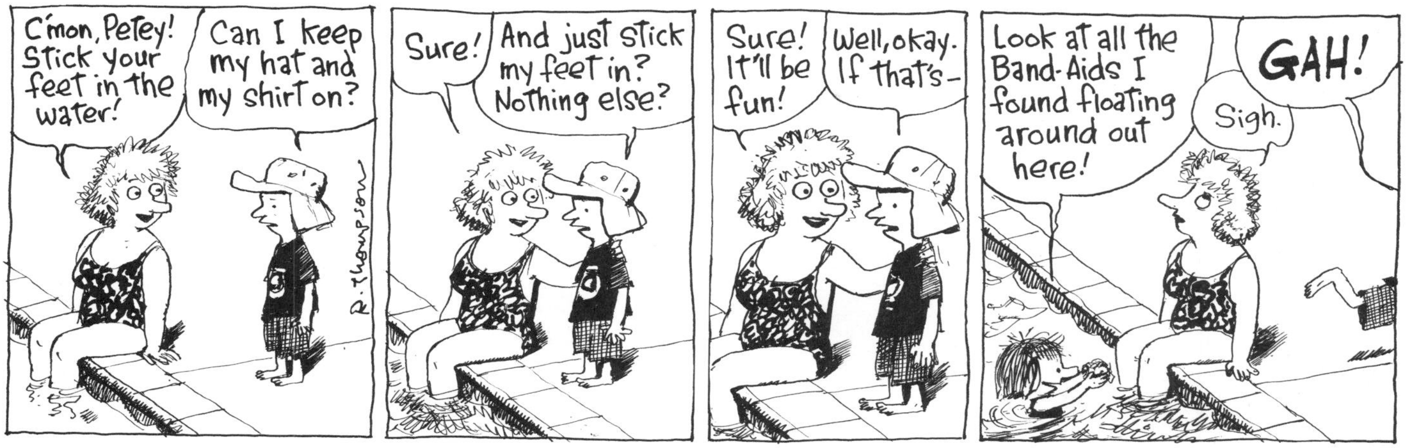
C'mon, Petey! Stick your feet in the water!
Can I keep my hat and my shirt on?
R. Thompson
Sure!
And just stick my feet in? Nothing else?
Sure! It'll be fun!
Well, okay. If that's–
Look at all the Band-Aids I found floating around out here!
Sigh.
GAH!

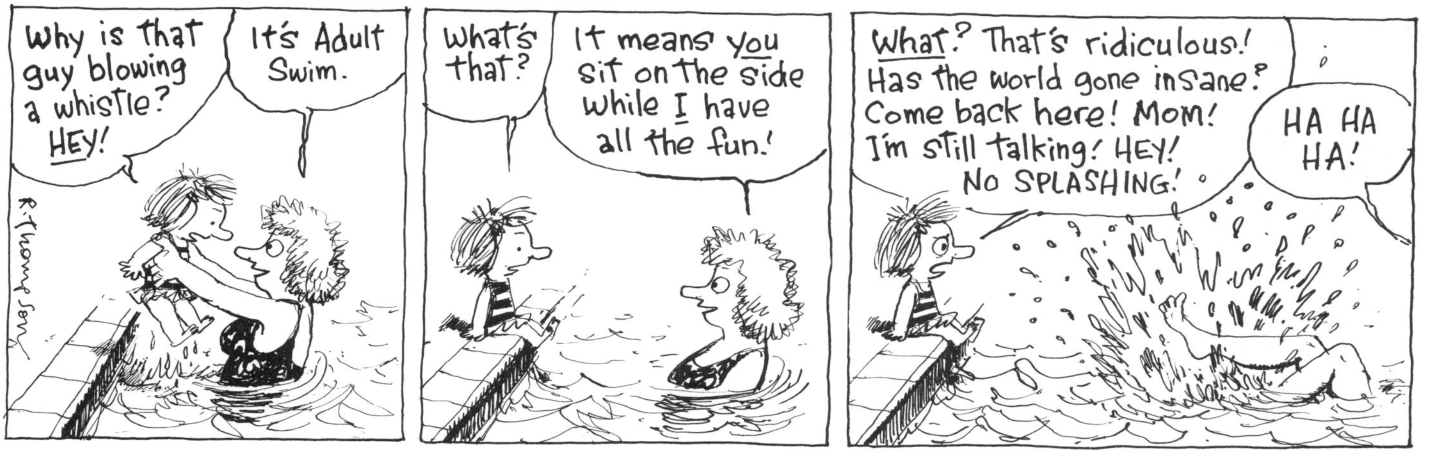
Why is that guy blowing a whistle? HEY!
It's Adult Swim.
R. Thompson
What's that?
It means you sit on the side while I have all the fun!
What? That's ridiculous! Has the world gone insane? Come back here! Mom! I'm still talking! HEY! NO SPLASHING!
HA HA HA!

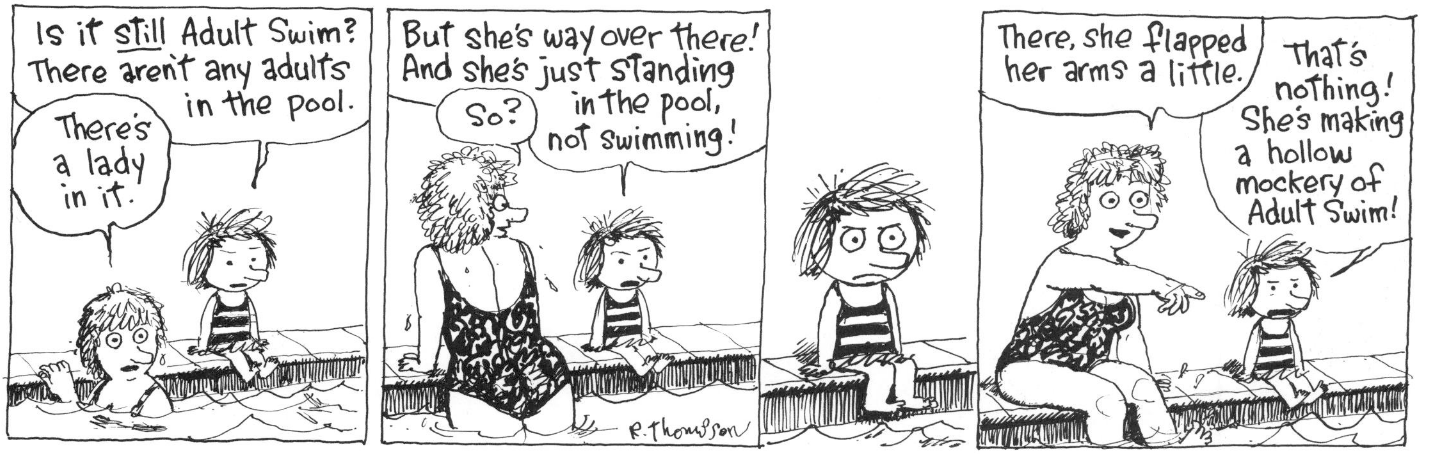
Is it still Adult Swim? There aren't any adults in the pool.
There's a lady in it.
But she's way over there! And she's just standing in the pool, not swimming!
So?
R. Thompson
There, she flapped her arms a little.
That's nothing! She's making a hollow mockery of Adult Swim!

Butterflies are so pretty.

Ah, but appearances can be deceptive.

Have you heard of the Butterfly Effect?

No.

What are they teaching kids these days?

It's the theory that a thing as small as the beat of a butterfly's wings can influence vast global weather systems.

Thus, my slightest gesture, my merest lazy twitch, could summon tornadoes, hurricanes, droughts, freak rains of frogs!

Uh.

HA! Think of the POWER! WHAT ROUGH BEAST FLUTTERS IN YON FIELD? IT IS I, BRINGER OF CATASTRO—

SQUISH.

What—

IT WAS SELF-DEFENSE, I SWEAR.

Over the years I've gotten a little leery of talking animals. They're freer of convention than those characters who are merely human, and they can unbalance a strip in their favor pretty easily. Thus Mr. Danders has disappeared for a little while. But if I impose a loosely enforced law that Everything Talks to Alice (as she's the center of the universe) then I can have an occasional talking animal. Such as this malevolent butterfly.

What is that?

Belgian llama cheese. I bought it at the Allfoods Market.

Oh, that place. They're always so serious there.

Yeah. It cost 12 bucks. Smell it.

YEEGHK!

I was hoping it'd be good. Phooey.

You've got cheese-buyer's remorse?

I do. It's sad.

MOLD

Oh boy! A Fuzzikin interactive pet like on TV! I'm going to name her Elspeth! Thanks, Dad!

It's going to smell up her room.

But it's not a total loss!

Again, cheese is funny.

My yard is full of those things, and I don't think they're flowers.

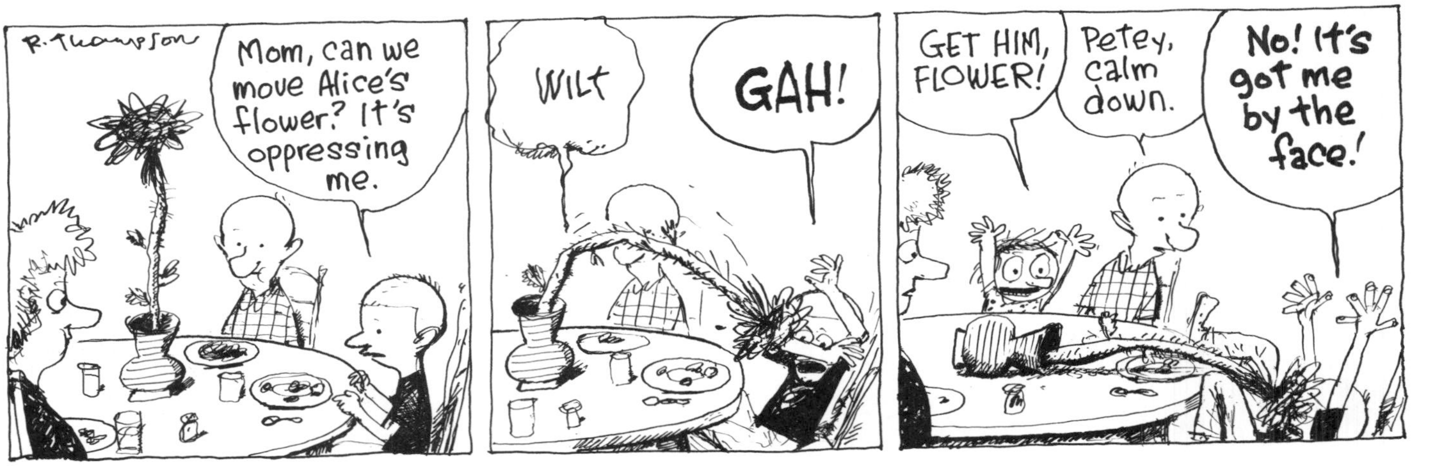
R. Thompson
Mom, can we move Alice's flower? It's oppressing me.
WILT
GAH!
GET HIM, FLOWER!
Petey, calm down.
No! It's got me by the face!

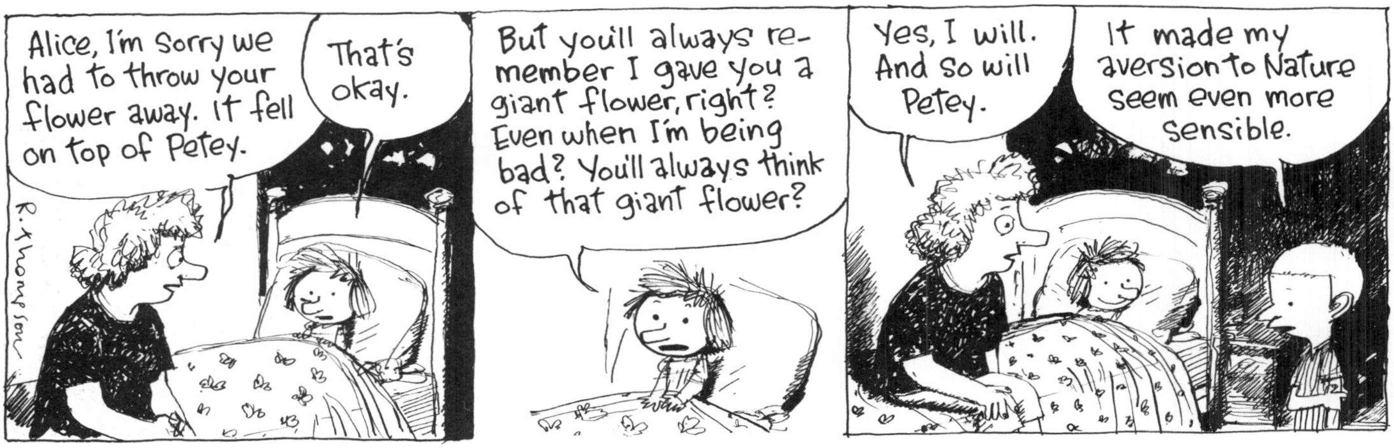
Alice, I'm sorry we had to throw your flower away. It fell on top of Petey.
That's okay.
R. Thompson
But you'll always remember I gave you a giant flower, right? Even when I'm being bad? You'll always think of that giant flower?
Yes, I will. And so will Petey.
It made my aversion to Nature seem even more sensible.

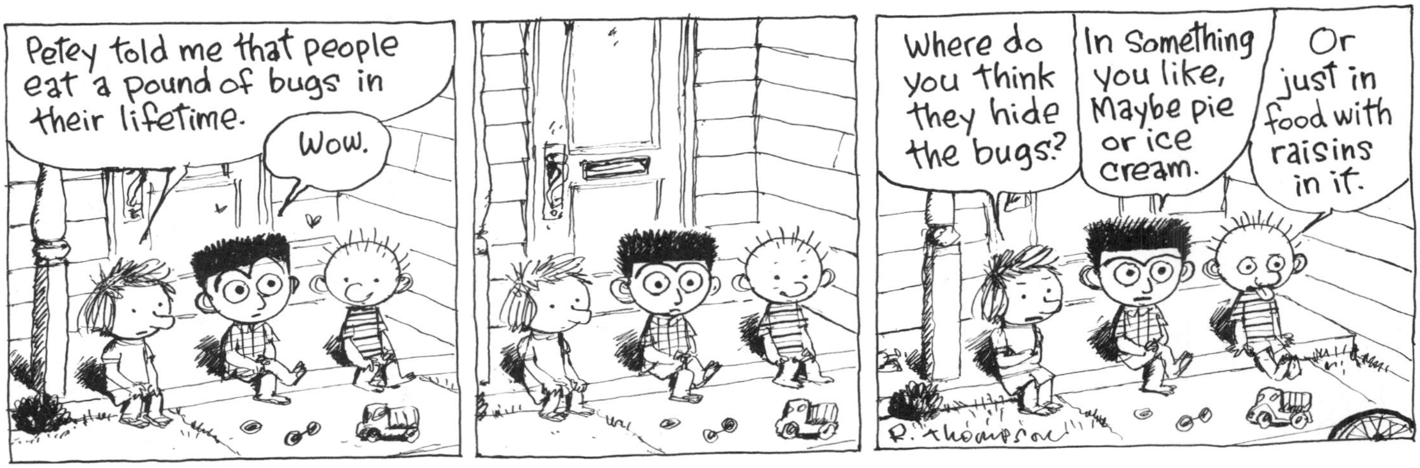
Petey told me that people eat a pound of bugs in their lifetime.
Wow.
Where do you think they hide the bugs?
In something you like, Maybe pie or ice cream.
Or just in food with raisins in it.
R. Thompson

The coming of the Uh-Oh Baby.

The Uh-Oh Baby is based on something I saw while waiting in line at a fancy ice-cream store. A woman with a little girl had ordered a complicated ice-cream cone that was taking the guy behind the counter awhile to construct.

When the cone finally appeared it was dazzling, an ornate thing in a waffle cone decked out with all kinds of jimmies and sprinkles. The woman took it and handed it down to her little girl, who immediately dropped it on the floor.

Everybody in the store froze in place, shocked by the shattered, ruined spread on the floor. The little girl, unfazed, put her palms up and said, "Uh-oh," like that's what we say when things go south.

OK, so it's not much of an anecdote. And I don't even like ice cream that much. But I'm sure there's a lesson for us all in there somewhere.

We had a guinea pig for a year or so. It was a former kindergarten classroom pet, rejected because of allergy issues.

After a year we gave it away to friends. It was not an impressive animal. It squeaked all night and the cats were scared of it.

This may be the first time that the legend of Robert Johnson was crossed with produce. Somebody pointed out to me that there are three stories going on here without it becoming confusing. If I could've, I would've made it four.

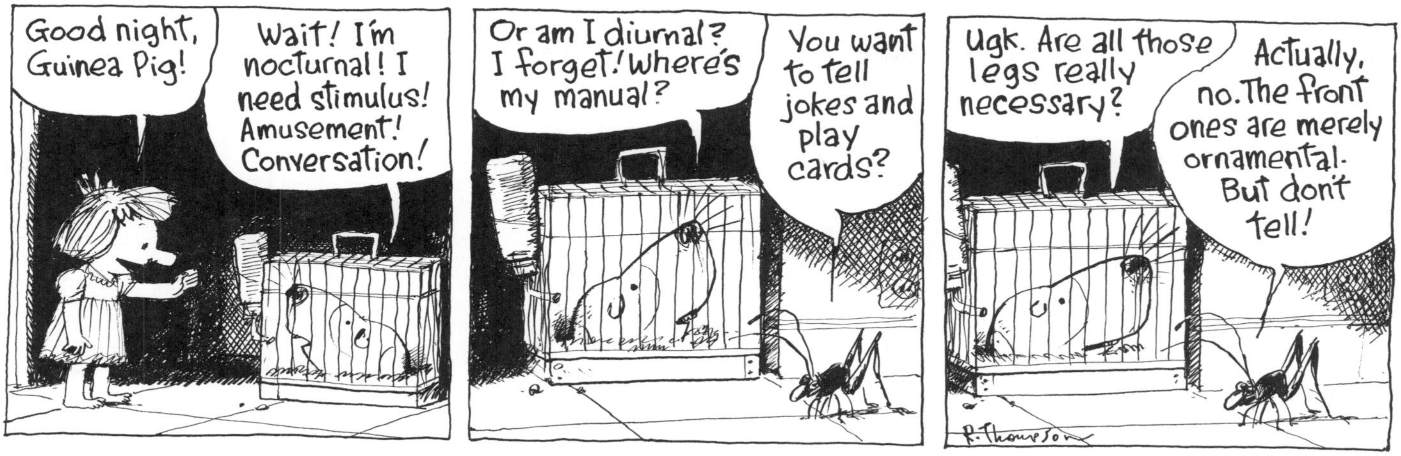
Good night, Guinea Pig!
Wait! I'm nocturnal! I need stimulus! Amusement! Conversation!
Or am I diurnal? I forget! Where's my manual?
You want to tell jokes and play cards?
Ugk. Are all those legs really necessary?
Actually, no. The front ones are merely ornamental. But don't tell!
R. Thompson

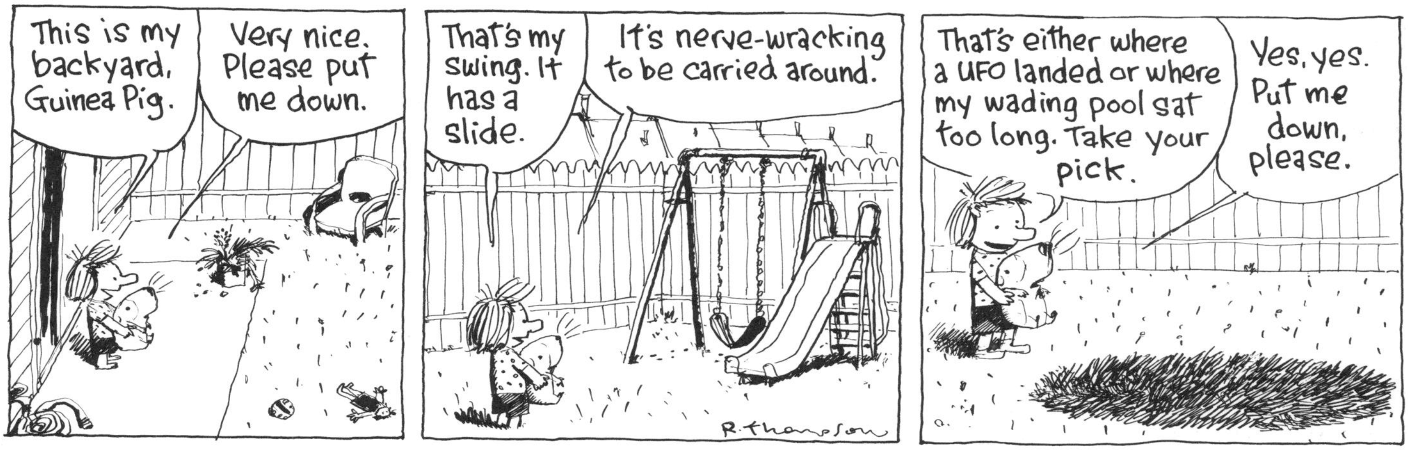
This is my backyard, Guinea Pig.
Very nice. Please put me down.
That's my swing. It has a slide.
It's nerve-wracking to be carried around.
R. Thompson
That's either where a UFO landed or where my wading pool sat too long. Take your pick.
Yes, yes. Put me down, please.

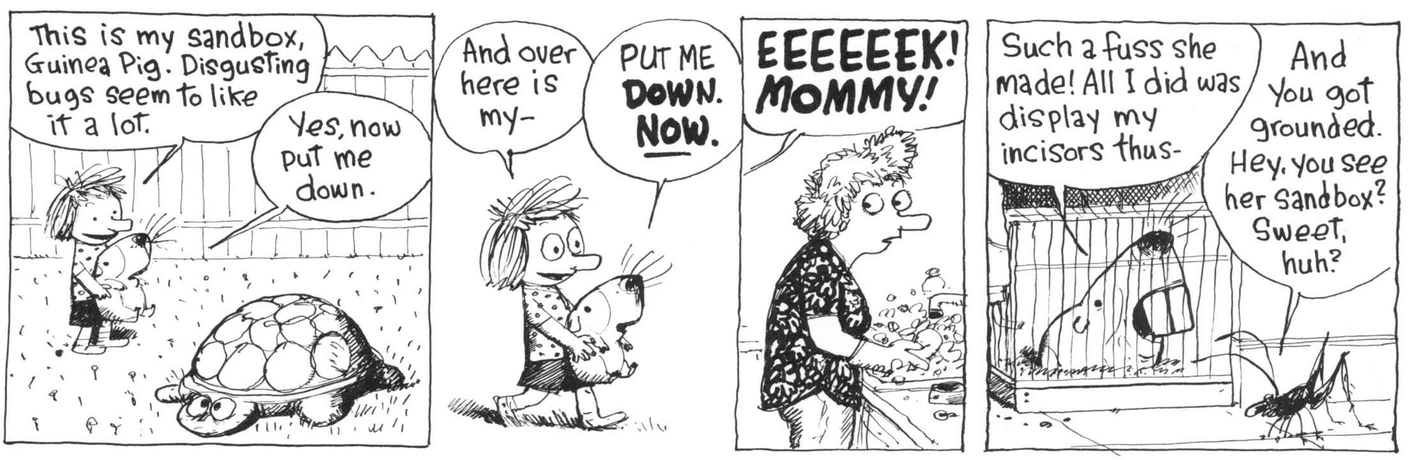
This is my sandbox, Guinea Pig. Disgusting bugs seem to like it a lot.
Yes, now put me down.
And over here is my–
PUT ME DOWN. NOW.
EEEEEEK! MOMMY!
Such a fuss she made! All I did was display my incisors thus–
And you got grounded. Hey, you see her sandbox? Sweet, huh?

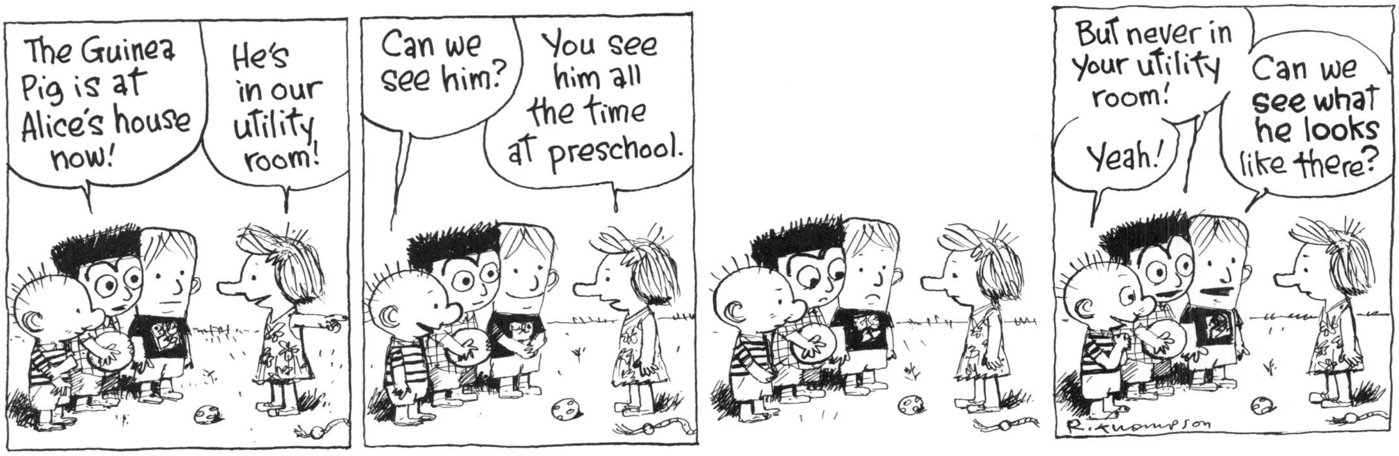
The Guinea Pig is at Alice's house now!
He's in our utility room!
Can we see him?
You see him all the time at preschool.
But never in your utility room!
Yeah!
Can we see what he looks like there?

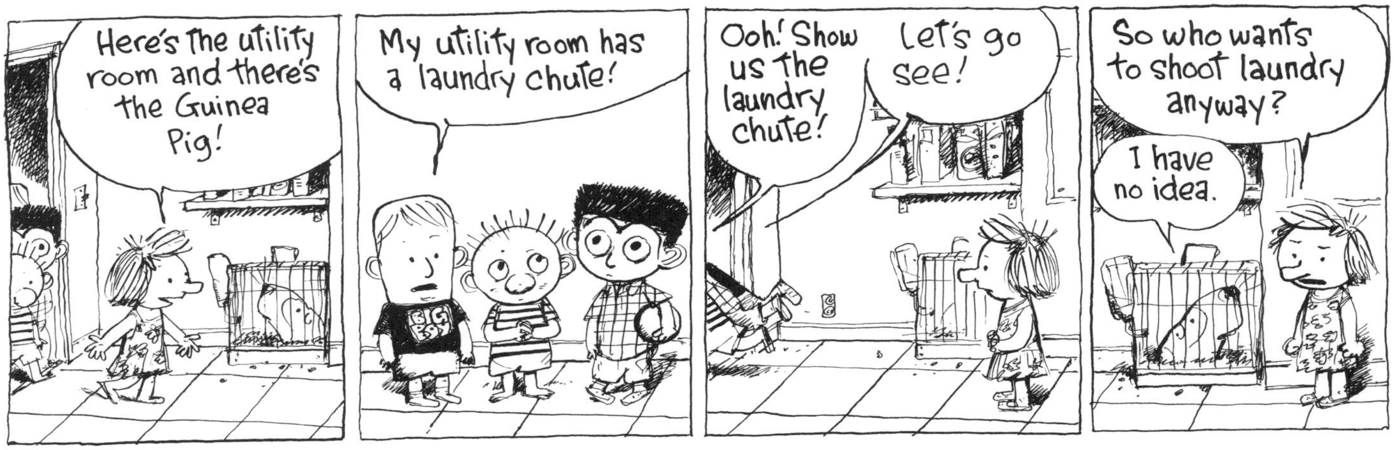
Here's the utility room and there's the Guinea Pig!
My utility room has a laundry chute!
Ooh! Show us the laundry chute!
Let's go see!
So who wants to shoot laundry anyway?
I have no idea.

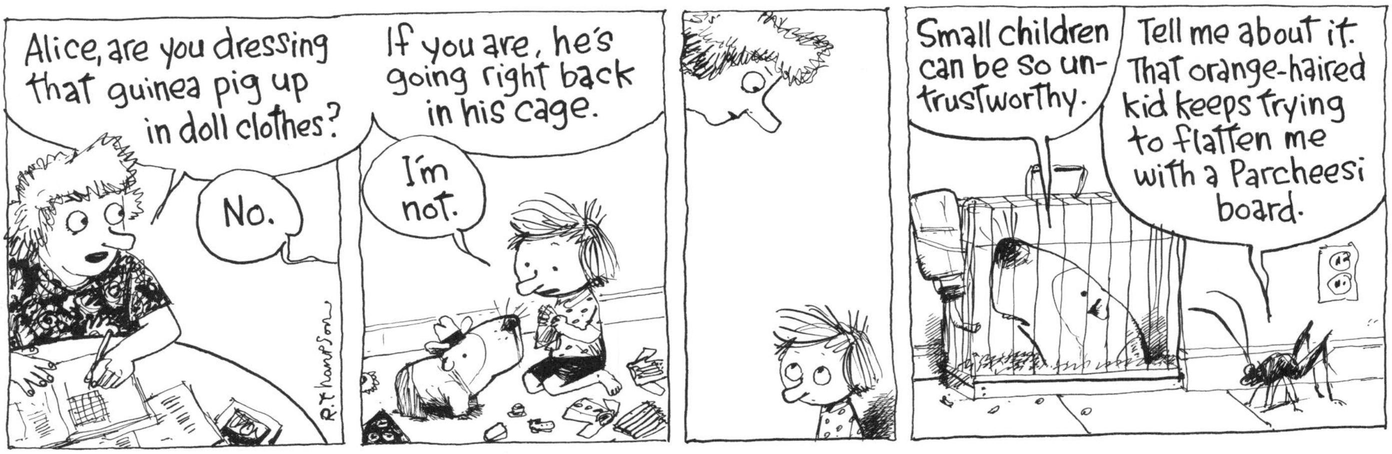
Alice, are you dressing that guinea pig up in doll clothes?
No.
If you are, he's going right back in his cage.
I'm not.
Small children can be so untrustworthy.
Tell me about it. That orange-haired kid keeps trying to flatten me with a Parcheesi board.

I think Dill's parents are former hippies who lived on a farm, and then moved their large family to the more confined space of a suburban neighborhood, but continued to think in the sprawlier ways of a farm. In other words, their yard is full of junk.

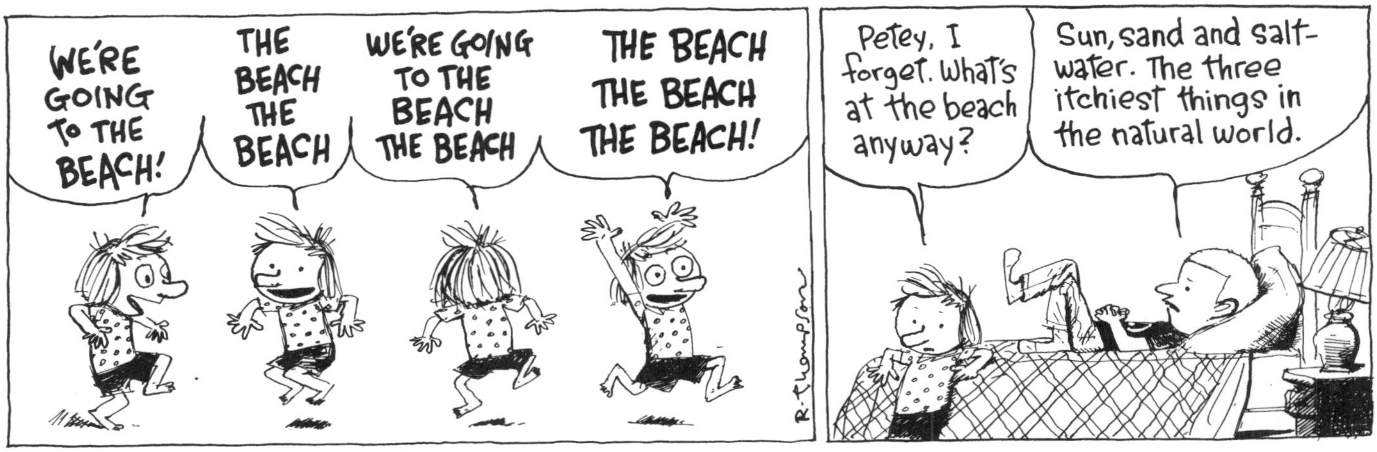
WE'RE GOING TO THE BEACH!
THE BEACH THE BEACH THE BEACH
WE'RE GOING TO THE BEACH THE BEACH
THE BEACH THE BEACH THE BEACH!
Petey, I forget. What's at the beach anyway?
Sun, sand and salt-water. The three itchiest things in the natural world.

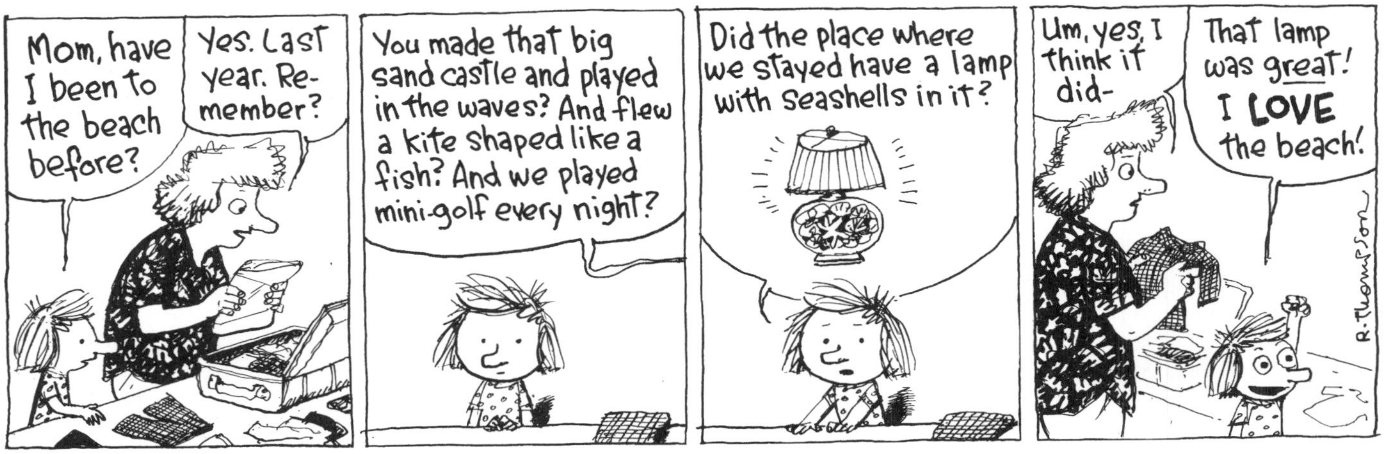
Mom, have I been to the beach before?
Yes. Last year. Re-member?
You made that big sand castle and played in the waves? And flew a kite shaped like a fish? And we played mini-golf every night?
Did the place where we stayed have a lamp with seashells in it?
Um, yes, I think it did-
That lamp was great! I LOVE the beach!

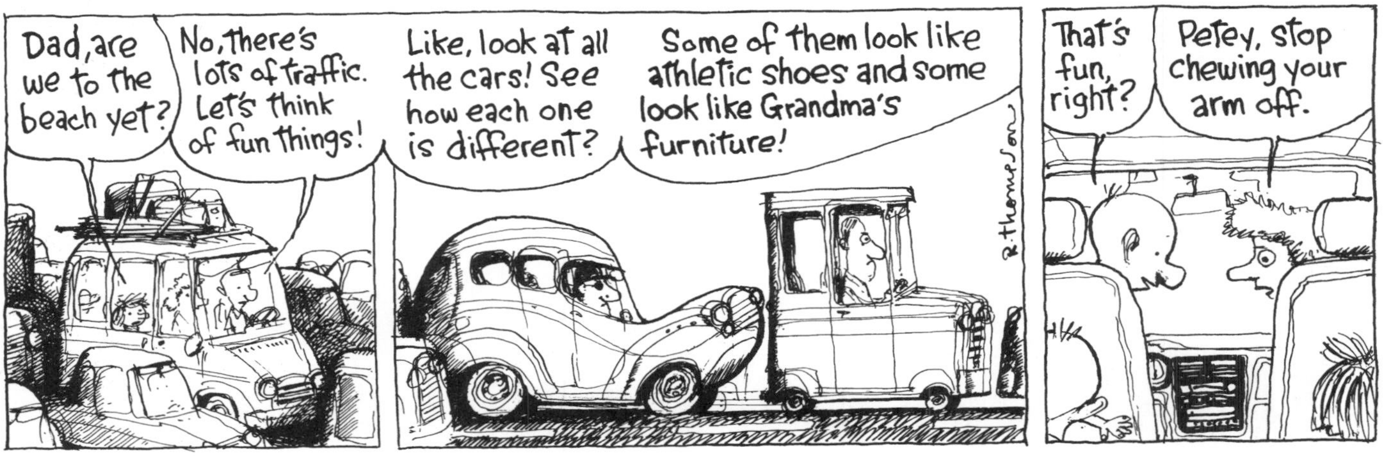
Dad, are we to the beach yet?
No, there's lots of traffic. Let's think of fun things!
Like, look at all the cars! See how each one is different?
Some of them look like athletic shoes and some look like Grandma's furniture!
That's fun, right?
Petey, stop chewing your arm off.

This might be proof that Ernesto is not imaginary. Or, as Petey believes, it might be evidence that he's a mass delusion.

This series was drawn at an actual beach house on the Outer Banks of North Carolina, so it's extra-accurate.

152

The center panel is another bow to *Little Nemo*. In one very famous episode, Nemo was carried away by his bed, which sprinted down the street on elongated legs.

Water and its movement is fun to draw. So are clouds and small children. If it weren't for the spit joke, this strip would be just too dang sweet.

That's a nice sand castle you've built, Alice.

It's not a castle. It's a shopping mall.

See, there are all the stores and where you're standing is the parking lot.

You're not going to play in the sand with Alice?

She's too advanced for me.

See the jellyfish? They sometimes wash up on shore.

Ooh!

I think it's plastic.

It says not to put this bag over your head in English, Spanish, German, French, Russian...

Oh.

And Japanese.

Who knew jellyfish spoke so many languages?

BLOAT

AGH

My comic book warped!

Humidity is nature's way of saying, "Petey, go play in the ocean."

The waves were drawn with a music staff pen. It's a nib with five points for ruling a music staff (duh), and it's great for making interesting textures when misused in a cartoon.

I forgot to draw the balloon around "ADULT SWIM" and I figure it's too late now.

155

This is pretty closely related to an old Sunday strip. Except here, Petey's opinion of mini-golf is more positive.

Pancakes!

Petey should dance more often.

Of all the creatures on God's green earth, cows are the second most fun to draw (elephants being the first).

The interior of a car, on the other hand, is difficult to draw. This one is adequate.

Gigantic, repulsive urns, however, are a joy to draw. Some days I give myself something fun to draw and some days something hard. Unless I'm feeling lazy; then it's all just talking heads.

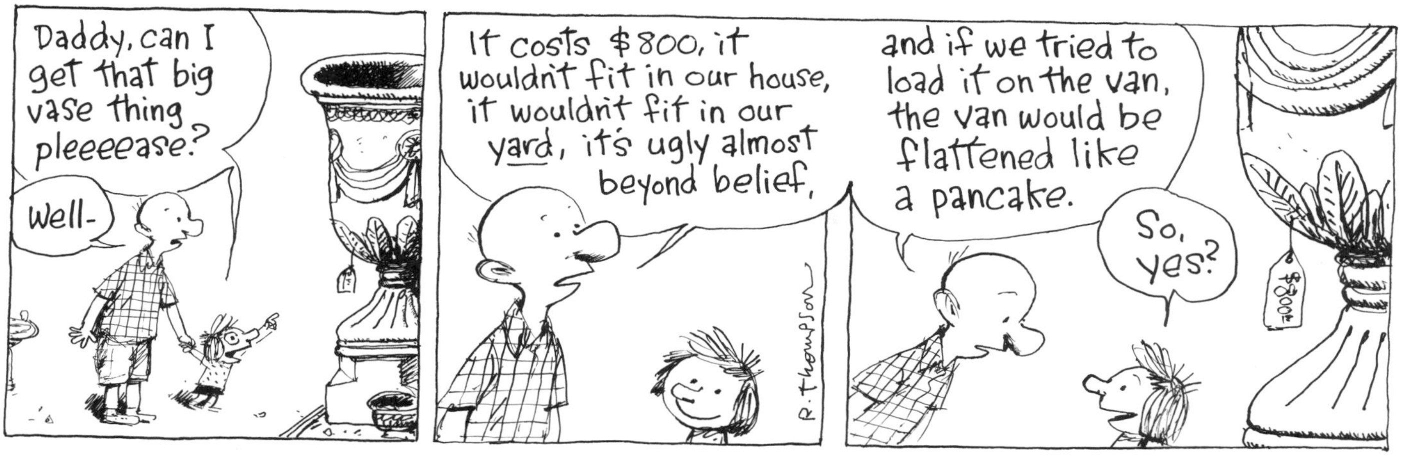
Daddy, can I get that big vase thing pleeeease?
Well-
It costs $800, it wouldn't fit in our house, it wouldn't fit in our yard, it's ugly almost beyond belief,
and if we tried to load it on the van, the van would be flattened like a pancake.
So, yes?

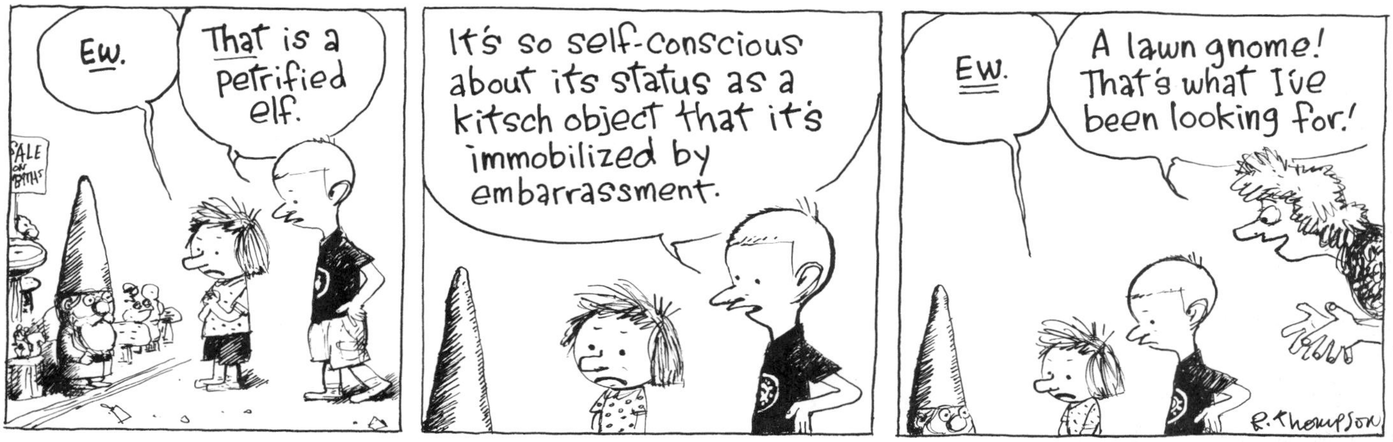
Ew.
That is a petrified elf.
It's so self-conscious about its status as a kitsch object that it's immobilized by embarrassment.
Ew.
A lawn gnome! That's what I've been looking for!

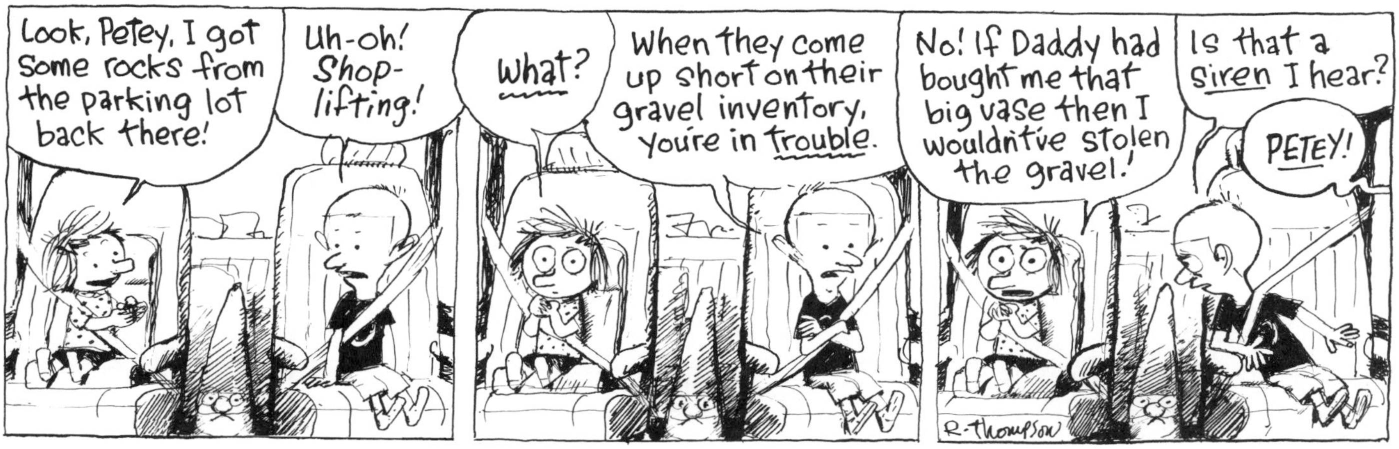
Look, Petey, I got some rocks from the parking lot back there!
Uh-oh! Shop-lifting!
What?
When they come up short on their gravel inventory, you're in trouble.
No! If Daddy had bought me that big vase then I wouldn't've stolen the gravel!
Is that a siren I hear?
PETEY!

Aw. A wise man said you can break hearts with a joke.

Note that Alice is peeking.

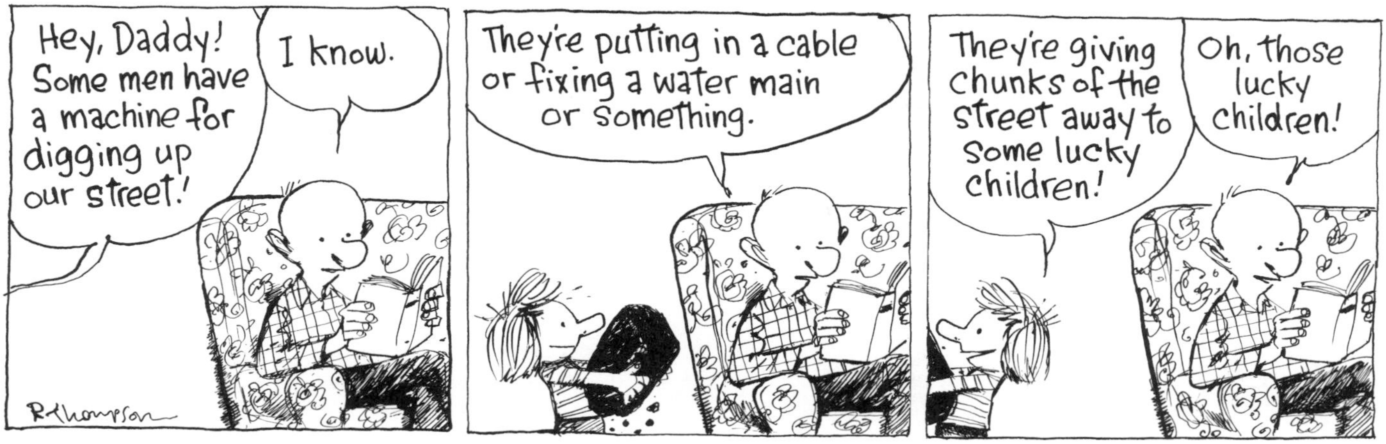
Hey, Daddy! Some men have a machine for digging up our street!
I know.
They're putting in a cable or fixing a water main or something.
They're giving chunks of the street away to some lucky children!
Oh, those lucky children!
R. Thompson

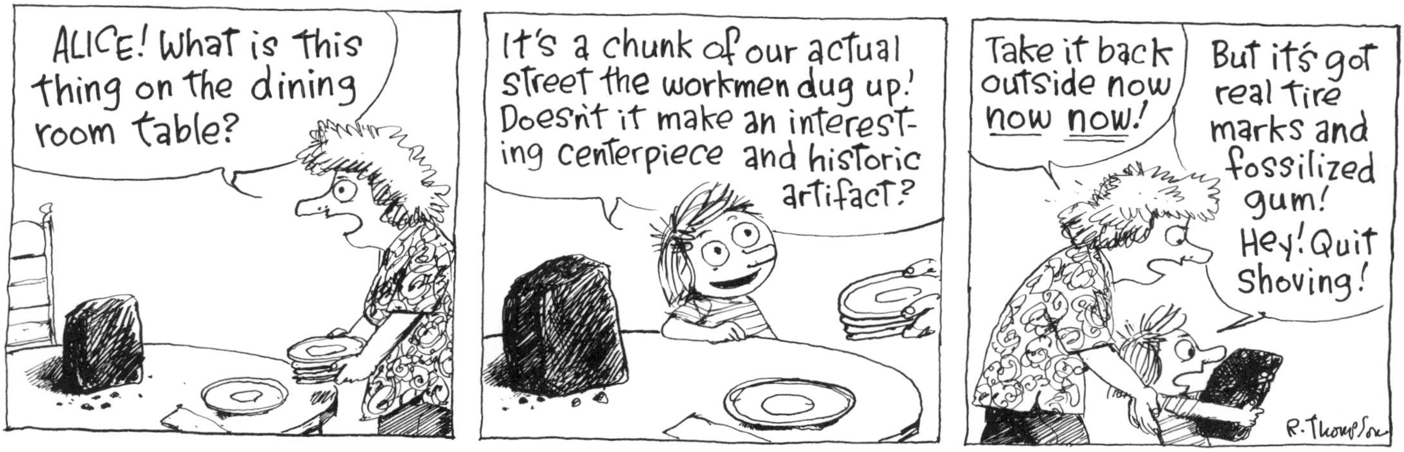
ALICE! What is this thing on the dining room table?
It's a chunk of our actual street the workmen dug up! Doesn't it make an interesting centerpiece and historic artifact?
Take it back outside now now now!
But it's got real tire marks and fossilized gum! Hey! Quit shoving!
R. Thompson

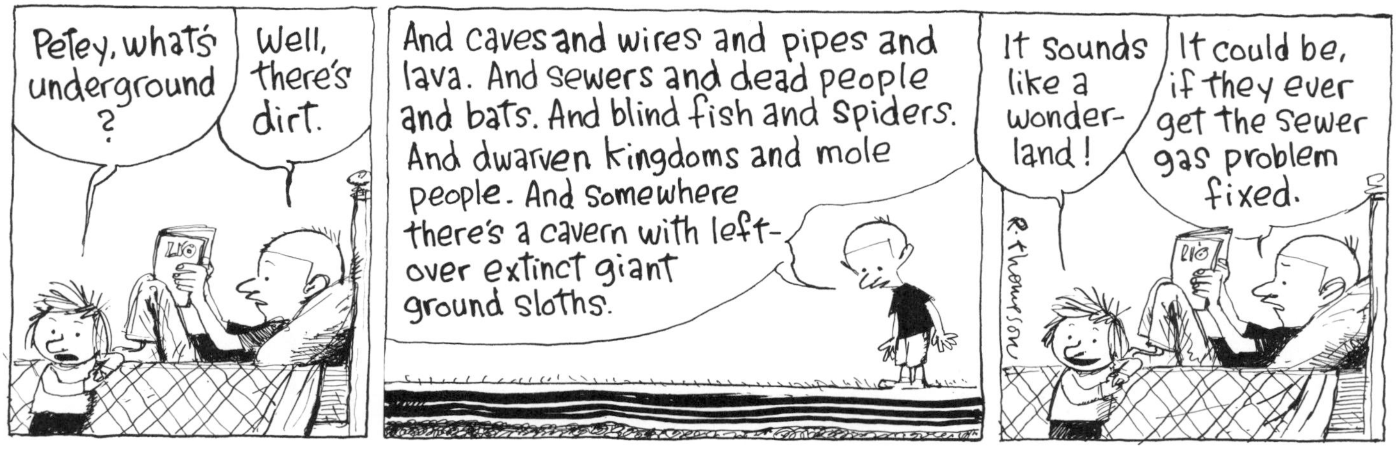
Petey, what's underground?
Well, there's dirt.
And caves and wires and pipes and lava. And sewers and dead people and bats. And blind fish and spiders. And dwarven kingdoms and mole people. And somewhere there's a cavern with left-over extinct giant ground sloths.
It sounds like a wonder-land!
It could be, if they ever get the sewer gas problem fixed.
R. Thompson

The bit about sea cucumbers is true. Most of Mr. Otterloop's comments are reliable; they're also rarely helpful.

Ernesto is in a hurry to grow up for all the wrong reasons. He knows adults have all the power and, being a Bond villain in embryo, he's a little power-crazed.

Alice! Your knee's bloody!

I *told* you that.

BL- BL- Oogh- Guh—

WUMP!

Hey.

Alice? What— which one of you needs help?

I was first in line, but you can start with Petey.

Oogh

R.Thompson

Ooh, what happened?

I fell down and you helped me up!

Huh?

But you fainted because my knee was all bloody. See?

AUGH! RELAPSE! RELAPSE!

Mom! A fresh damp towel for Petey!

What is it?

It's a shopping mall!

R.Thompson

Here's the daddy store, and the mommy store, and all the little children stores, and here's the food court where they eat!

I'll make a big box store for them to go shopping in.

Good idea!

Irresistible Force meets Incurable Optimism.

Every kid-based comic strip has a designated bully. In this one, it's Alice, unfortunately.

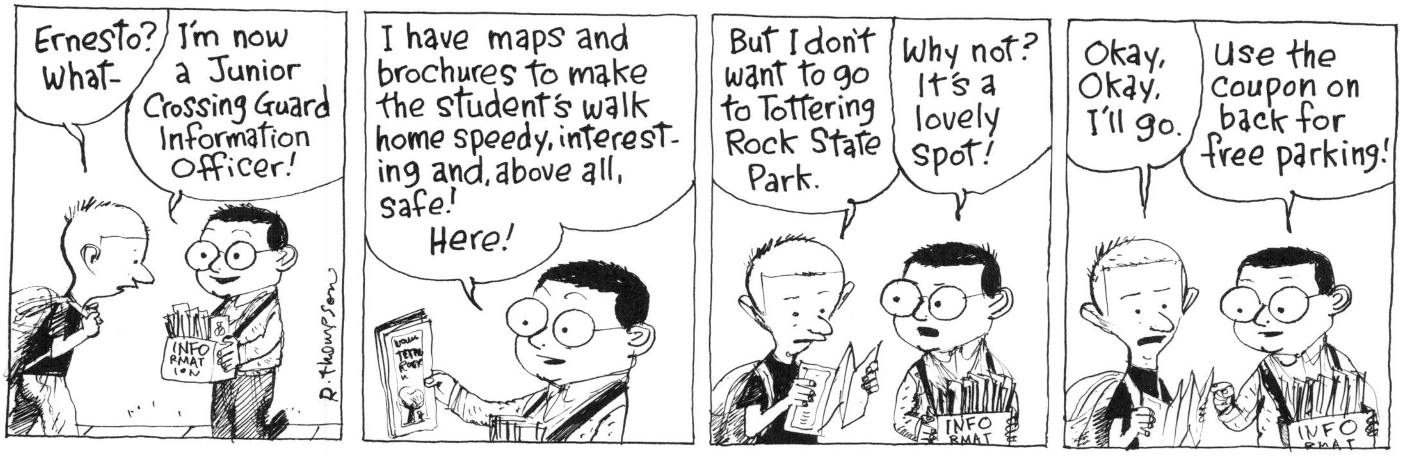
Ernesto? What-
I'm now a Junior Crossing Guard Information Officer!
INFO RMAT ION
R. Thompson
I have maps and brochures to make the student's walk home speedy, interesting and, above all, safe!
Here!
But I don't want to go to Tottering Rock State Park.
Why not? It's a lovely spot!
INFO RMAT
Okay, Okay, I'll go.
Use the coupon on back for free parking!

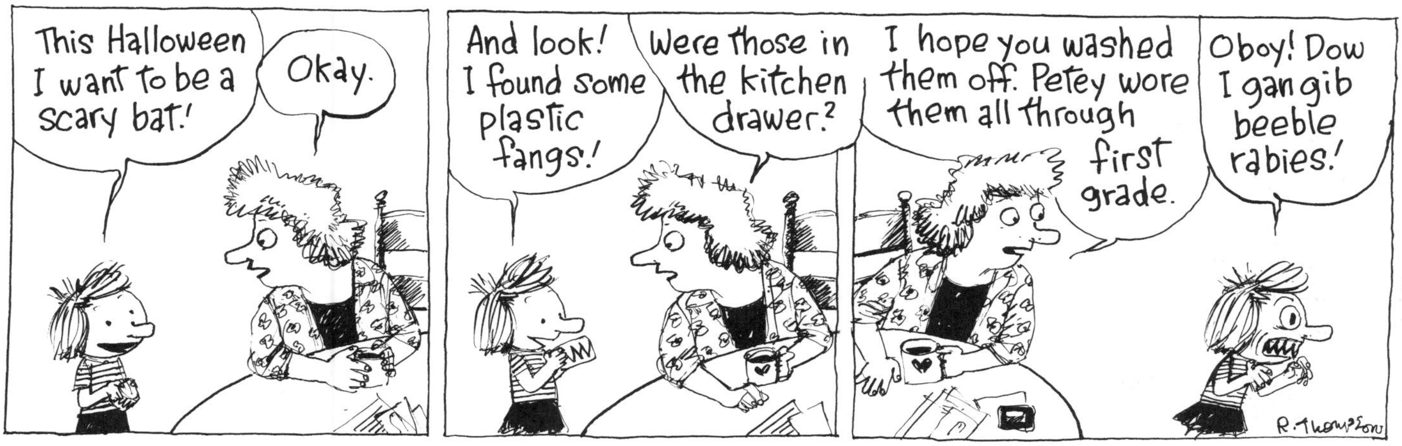
This Halloween I want to be a scary bat!
Okay.
And look! I found some plastic fangs!
Were those in the kitchen drawer?
I hope you washed them off. Petey wore them all through first grade.
Oboy! Dow I gan gib beeble rabies!
R. Thompson

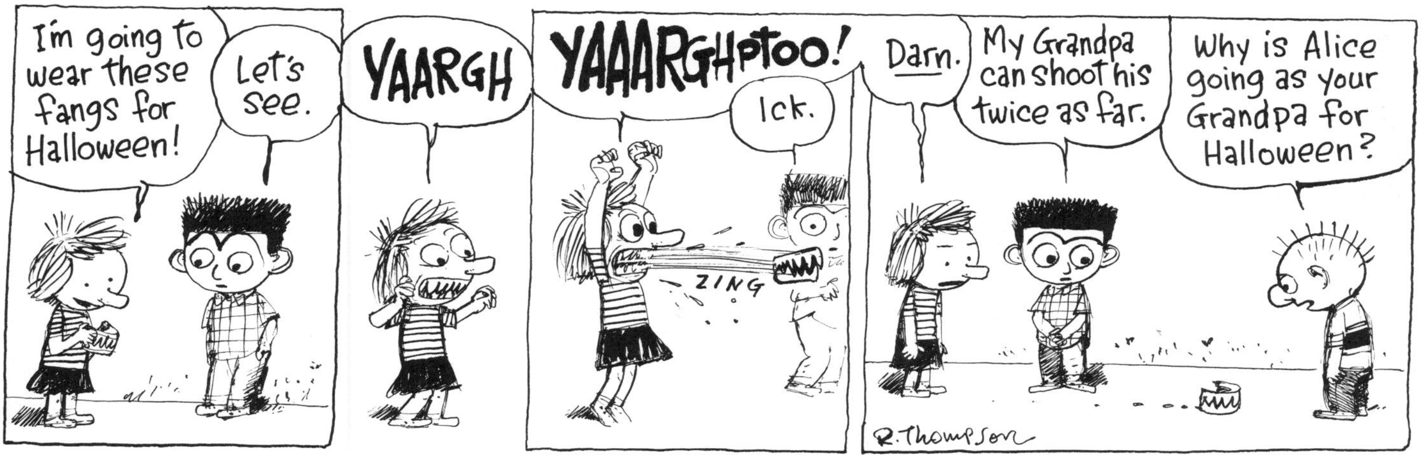
I'm going to wear these fangs for Halloween!
Let's see.
YAARGH
YAAARGHPTOO!
Ick.
ZING
Darn.
My Grandpa can shoot his twice as far.
Why is Alice going as your Grandpa for Halloween?
R. Thompson

Like I said, Dill's family moved to the suburbs from a farm. On a farm, there's room to do things: put up outbuildings, raise livestock, store machinery, haul things. And build trebuchets. These activities translate poorly to the little fraction of an acre available in suburban development houses, but it's fun to try.

Again, Dill is moved by the poignancy of the inanimate.

The Uh-Oh Baby should appear just often enough to make readers antsy at the appearance of a baby, any baby, in the strip.

I do this, too, but I'll never admit it. From what I've heard, most people do this but will never admit it.

Again with the cross-hatching. There's nothing like it for establishing atmosphere, or ruining your eyesight.

So, did you get lost at school today?

Yeah.

And the English teacher hooked her car up to her portable classroom and drove off to join the circus.

Why did she do that?

Word is the literacy rate among clowns is way down. I'm going to my room to read comic books now.

Whole caravans of portable classrooms have been sighted crossing the continent in search of school systems that are solvent and in need of qualified teachers.

Here are my sketches for my Halloween costume.

A hideous, revolting scary bat.

Who's also cute and fuzzy and, ideally, pink.

Horrifying yet adorable? Just like you?

Yes. Can you help me turn my vision into reality?

Here's my Halloween costume!

·Sip·

Ha ha! See? I put a box on my head! It's a subtle yet scathing commentary on our consumer culture!

Ha ha! Boy, this'll really shock some people! Ha ha ha ha!

I didn't get that at all, did you?

I thought he was being a square peg.

In a few years Ernesto will *rule* the Junior Crossing Guards and the whole nation will tremble under his dominion! Especially if the whole nation wants to cross the street.

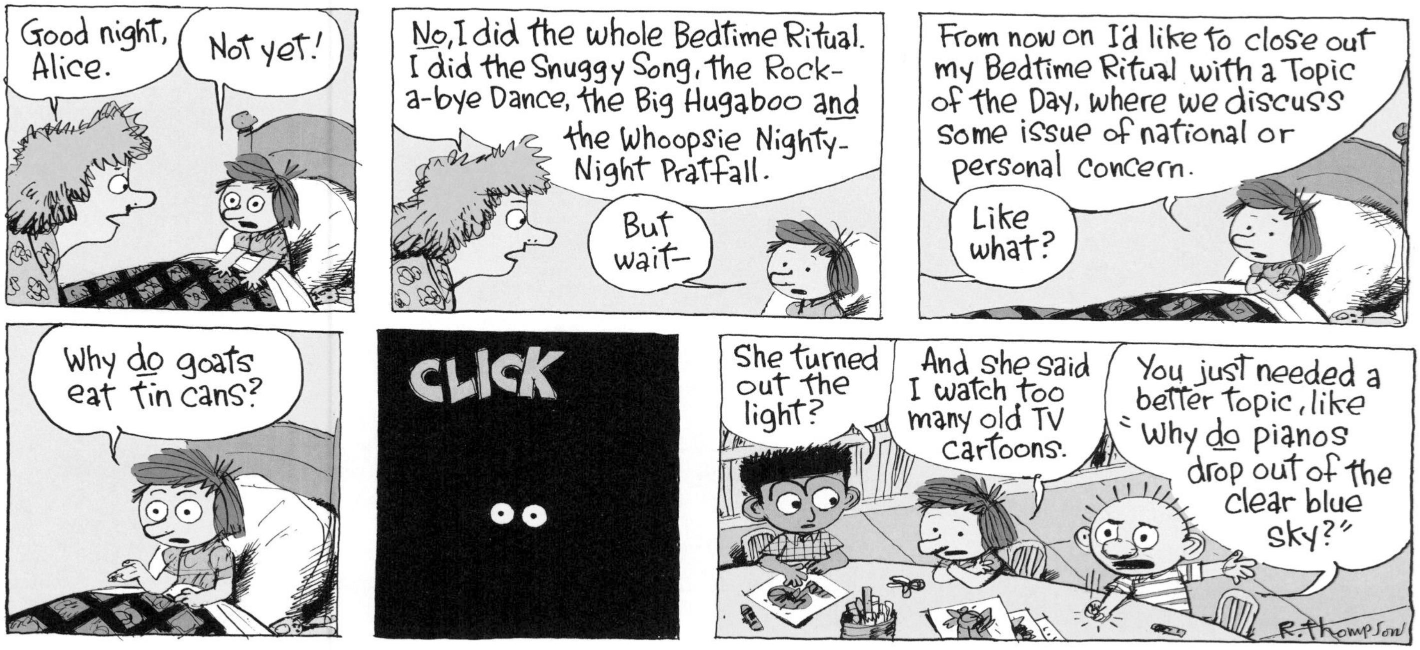
Good night, Alice.
Not yet!
No, I did the whole Bedtime Ritual. I did the Snuggy Song, the Rock-a-bye Dance, the Big Hugaboo and the Whoopsie Nighty-Night Pratfall.
But wait—
From now on I'd like to close out my Bedtime Ritual with a Topic of the Day, where we discuss some issue of national or personal concern.
Like what?
Why do goats eat tin cans?
CLICK
She turned out the light?
And she said I watch too many old TV cartoons.
You just needed a better topic, like "Why do pianos drop out of the clear blue sky?"
R. Thompson

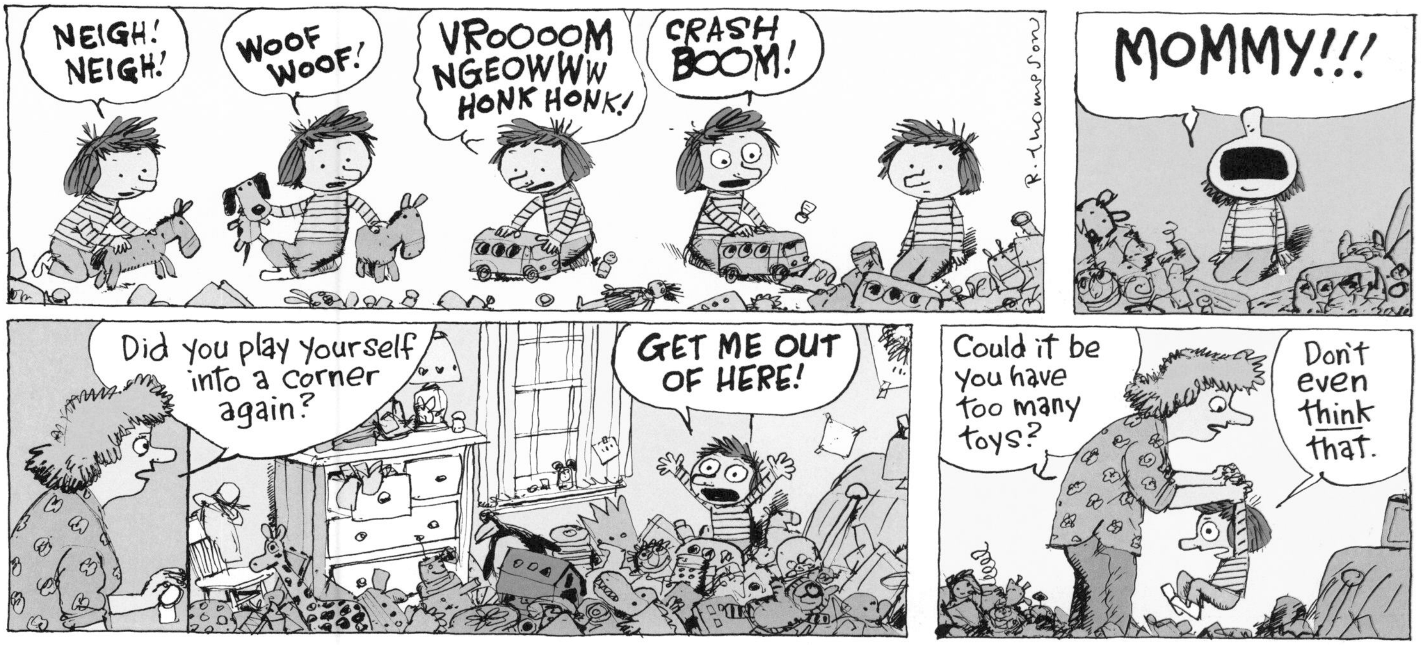
NEIGH! NEIGH!
WOOF WOOF!
VROOOOM NGEOWWW HONK HONK!
CRASH BOOM!
R. Thompson
MOMMY!!!
Did you play yourself into a corner again?
GET ME OUT OF HERE!
Could it be you have too many toys?
Don't even think that.

"Subtle" is a nice way of saying "incoherent." An editor once told me that a cartoon I'd drawn might be too subtle for his paper's readers, and I knew right away what he meant.

POGRIMBY. POGRIMBY. POGRIMBY. POGRIMBY. POG-RIM-BY. PO-GRIMBY. PO-GRIM-BY. POG-RIMBY. POGRIMBY POGRIMBY POGRIMBY POGRIMBY.

Ha-ha! My Dad is right! If you say a word too many times, it doesn't sound like a real word anymore!

Pogrimby isn't a real word.

You mean I destroyed it?

No, it—

What power you have! Try it with "oatmeal." I'd appreciate it.

Alice, you're not wearing the bat ears I made in the tub, are you?

No.

I hope not, 'cause they'd be ruined if they got wet.

Uh-oh.

Well. Instead of a bat, you can go as a basset hound for Halloween.

How did this happen?

There. I made you some new bat ears. Don't ruin these. Okay?

Ha-ha! These are pink and fuzzy!

The first ears you made were insufficiently pink and fuzzy, so their destruction in the bathtub was actually all for the best!

Right, Mom?! Right? Mom? Hey, come back.

I've heard of the legendary Poodle-Bat, but never dreamed I'd actually see it!

Marcus would get a lot of pity candy, too.

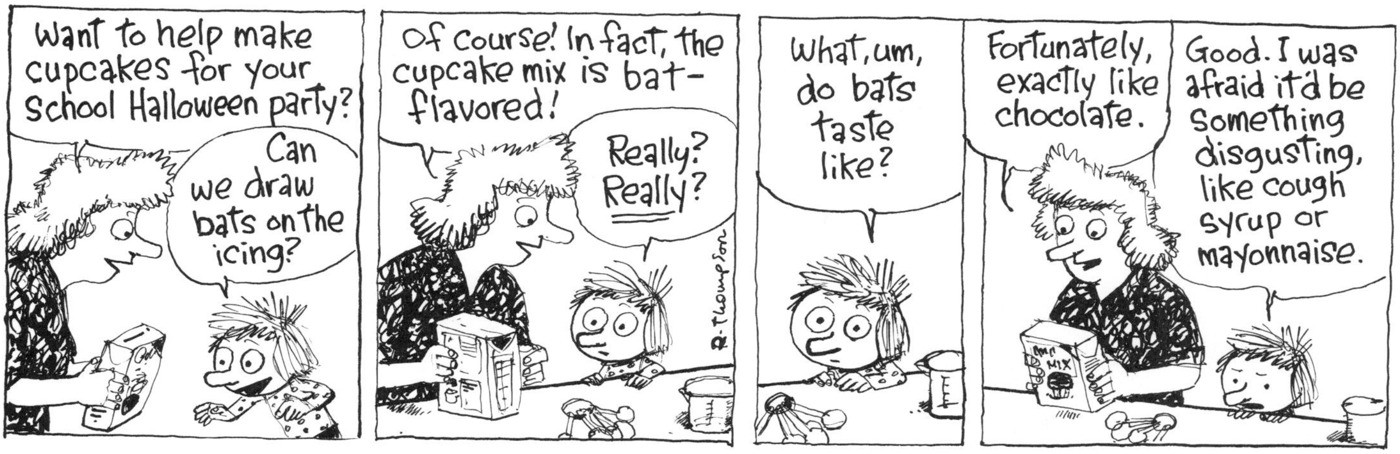
Want to help make cupcakes for your School Halloween party?
Can we draw bats on the icing?
Of course! In fact, the cupcake mix is bat-flavored!
Really? Really?
What, um, do bats taste like?
Fortunately, exactly like chocolate.
Good. I was afraid it'd be something disgusting, like cough syrup or mayonnaise.

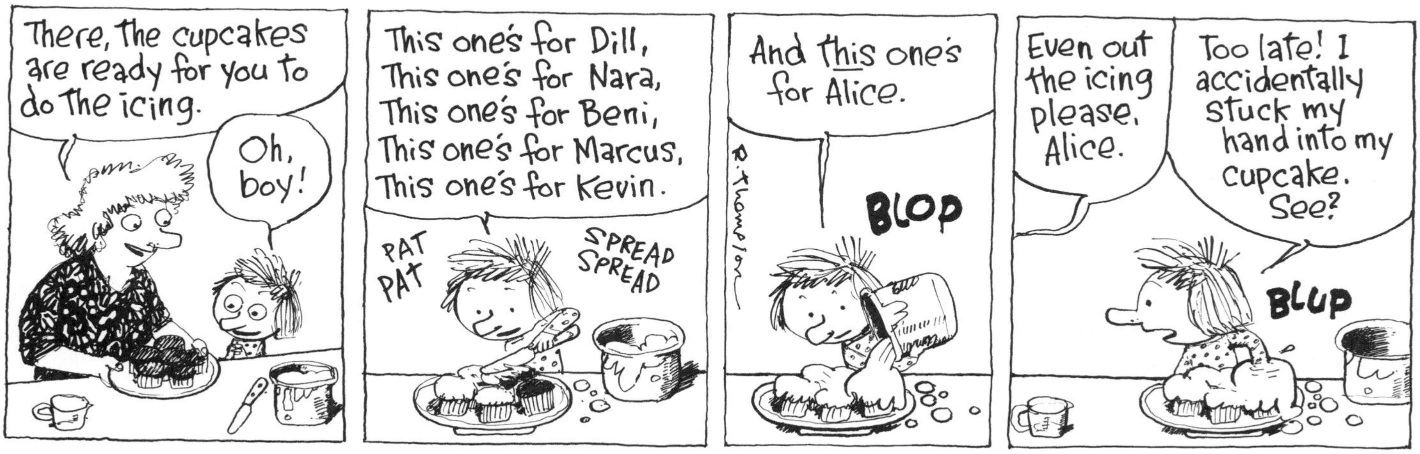
There, the cupcakes are ready for you to do the icing.
Oh, boy!
This one's for Dill, This one's for Nara, This one's for Beni, This one's for Marcus, This one's for Kevin.
PAT PAT
SPREAD SPREAD
And this one's for Alice.
BLOP
Even out the icing please, Alice.
Too late! I accidentally stuck my hand into my cupcake. See?
BLUP

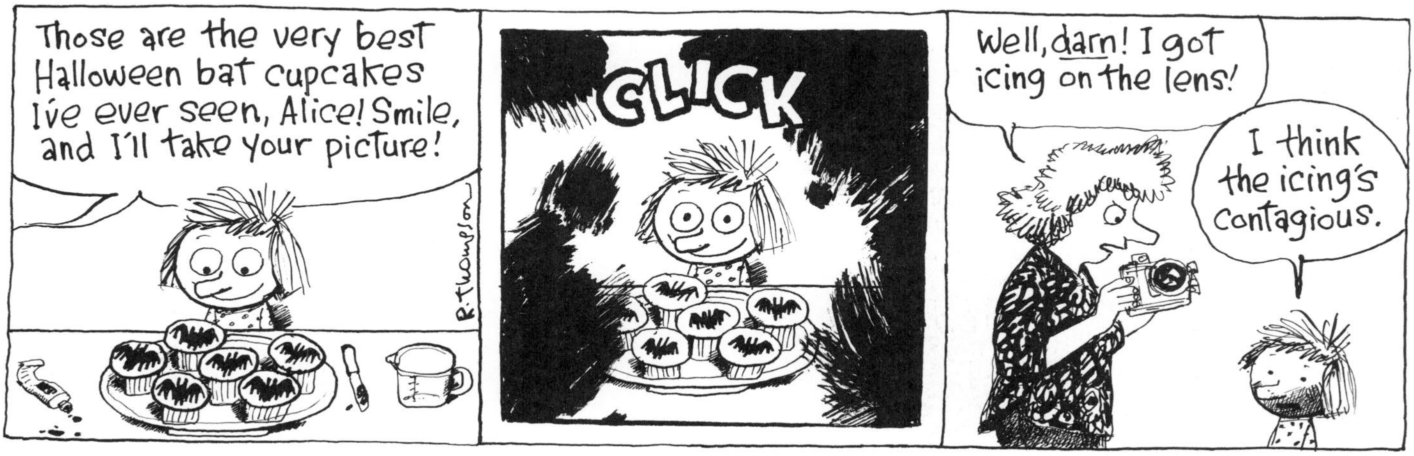
Those are the very best Halloween bat cupcakes I've ever seen, Alice! Smile, and I'll take your picture!
CLICK
Well, darn! I got icing on the lens!
I think the icing's contagious.

Maybe comics appeal so strongly to Petey because of his control-freakishness. He's right about film's passivity versus comic's engagement. And Alice is definitely right about that actor eyeball thing. But, having said all that, do comic books still run ads for whoopee cushions?

Pulling back suddenly in the sixth and seventh panels after the flatness of the preceding five gives this strip a dramatic depth of field not seen since *Citizen Kane*, I'll bet.

Panel 1: I made cupcakes for our party, Miss Bliss! / Ooh! Please put them on the table, Alice.

Panel 2: BEHOLD! The most awesome Halloween cupcakes ever made! / FLING

Panel 3: There's no icing! / The icing is all stuck to the plastic wrap. / EEK.

Panel 4: AAAAW OOOH HOOO! / Man, is that sad / Let's go sit in the rocking chair, Alice.

Spraying the cling wrap with oil would've prevented this, I've since learned.

 Daddy'll be out in a minute to take you trick-or-treating. / Okay, Mom.

 Do you think that sometimes Mom's kinda vivid? / Does "vivid" mean "loud"?

 HEE HEE HEE! WHERE ARE SOME CHILDREN I CAN FATTEN UP WITH CANDY?

 HEE HEE HEE! / Yes. / Yes.

 How did your trick-or-treating go? / Terrible! The cuteness of my costume barely registered with people.

 It's because Petey confused people with that dumb box on his head! / I kept explaining that I was a scathing commentary on our consumer culture.

 Instead of candy, they gave me political campaign literature. / Ick. / Meanwhile, they ignored the cute little girl in the bat costume.

The jungle gym looks bigger.

It's growing.

It grows during the night. One day it'll cover the planet, and we'll live in a giant jungle gym.

Then my Dad will commute to work by tube slide!

Haha! I bet he rips his pants!

Hey! I was still playing with that.

You put it down for five seconds. I get it now.

No, the five-second rule means you have to eat it.

I'm not going to eat it! You're thinking of the ten-second rule!

No, the ten-second rule means "Stop what you're doing before I count to ten or there will be consequences."

Or is that the two-minute warning?

Oh, take the dumb toy! I don't have time for this!

Time and numbers must be confusing to four year olds, and a little threatening.

All the toys at this preschool are old and broken.

They're relics of the many ancient civilizations that have dwelled at Blisshaven.

Like this Pull-and-Talk toy.

GNAH GNOGG SHAEZZZ BOWOW OWOWOW ONGHH ONG-

That's how people in ancient times talked.

No wonder I don't understand my parents.

Stuffing jokes are cheap and easy, though not as cheap or easy as fruitcake jokes.

Peter! You'll be glad to hear that I've been named principal trombonist of the school band!

Yeah? I'm playing oboe—

Once, on a television cartoon, I saw a cat put a boxing glove on a trombone slide with most intriguing results. Would you know where I could find a boxing glove?

Gee, no. I—

You don't? Pity. Well, my music teacher **seems** hesitant about the technique.

How about a cream pie? A cream pie might work.

Petey originally played the trombone, as I said, because it's loud and aggressive in an elbow-throwing way. Therefore, it's counterintuitive to Petey's character and thus it's funny. Ernesto originally played the bassoon. Maybe after he pinched his finger in the bassoon case he went sour on bassoons and switched to the trombone.

I've been thinking about your Grandma and her giant dog.

So have I.

It reminds me of the story of Little Red Riding Hood, with the Grandma and the Wolf.

Only in your story, Grandma and the Wolf are in cahoots!

Oh, great.

Wow, if she gets the Three Bears on her side, you're in trouble.

The first step in making a handprint turkey is to carefully trace your hand on the paper plate.

And remember, Creativity plus Neatness equals Art.

Wow! Look at that! It's my hand! Ha ha.!

I hear that handprint turkeys are kept on file by the FBI to identify future criminals.

The Handprint of Alice! I almost hate to deface it with a stupid turkey.

Another example of Mr. Otterloop's clumsiness. He should probably not try anything more physical than a pat on the head, or somebody's going to get hurt.

Who invented the tooth fairy? How does she fit into childhood mythology? Did the ancient Greeks have a tooth fairy that the Romans swiped and renamed? Was the tooth fairy then co-opted by a more vital religious tradition so we have her today? Who knows?

Actually, I forgot about the plastic fangs when drawing the Halloween series and felt obligated to bring them back. Mistakes like that can pay off big later on if you pretend they're intentional.

The Otterloops spend more time reading printed material than fooling with the computer because books and newspapers are more fun to draw. I'd have them listening to LPs and wax cylinders for the same reason. As technology advances, it becomes less interesting to draw.

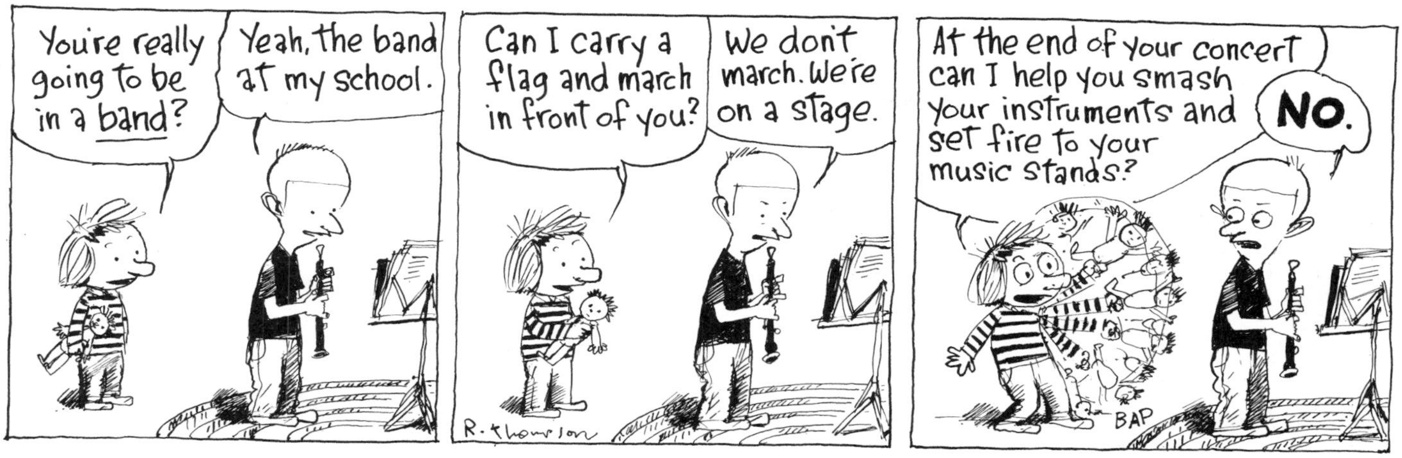
You're really going to be in a band?
Yeah, the band at my school.
Can I carry a flag and march in front of you?
We don't march. We're on a stage.
R. Thompson
At the end of your concert can I help you smash your instruments and set fire to your music stands?
NO.
BAP

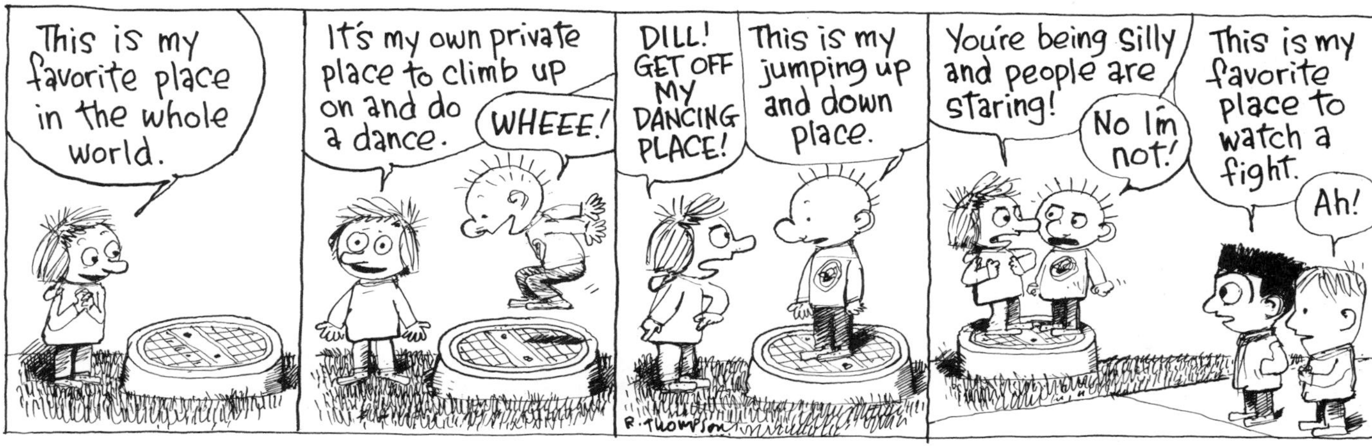
This is my favorite place in the whole world.
It's my own private place to climb up on and do a dance.
WHEEE!
DILL! GET OFF MY DANCING PLACE!
This is my jumping up and down place.
R. Thompson
You're being silly and people are staring!
No I'm not!
This is my favorite place to watch a fight.
Ah!

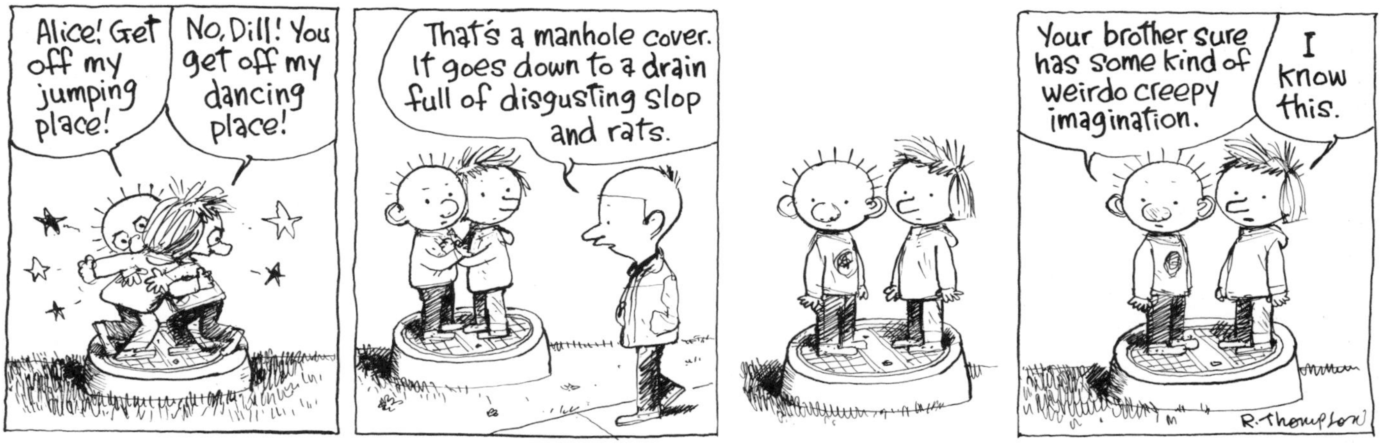
Alice! Get off my jumping place!
No, Dill! You get off my dancing place!
That's a manhole cover. It goes down to a drain full of disgusting slop and rats.
Your brother sure has some kind of weirdo creepy imagination.
I know this.
R. Thompson

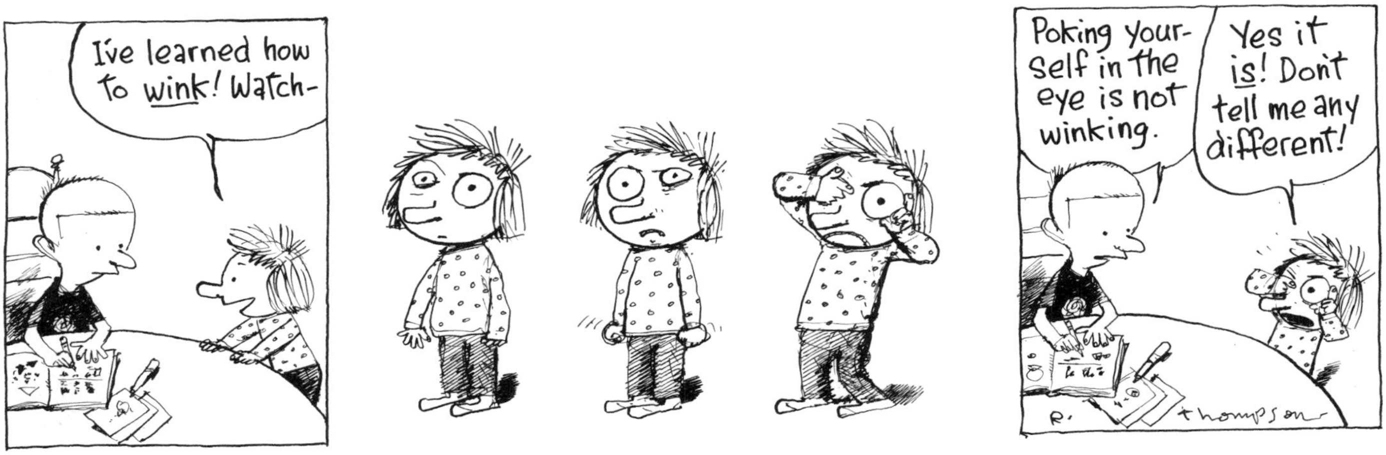
I've learned how to wink! Watch-
Poking yourself in the eye is not winking.
Yes it is! Don't tell me any different!

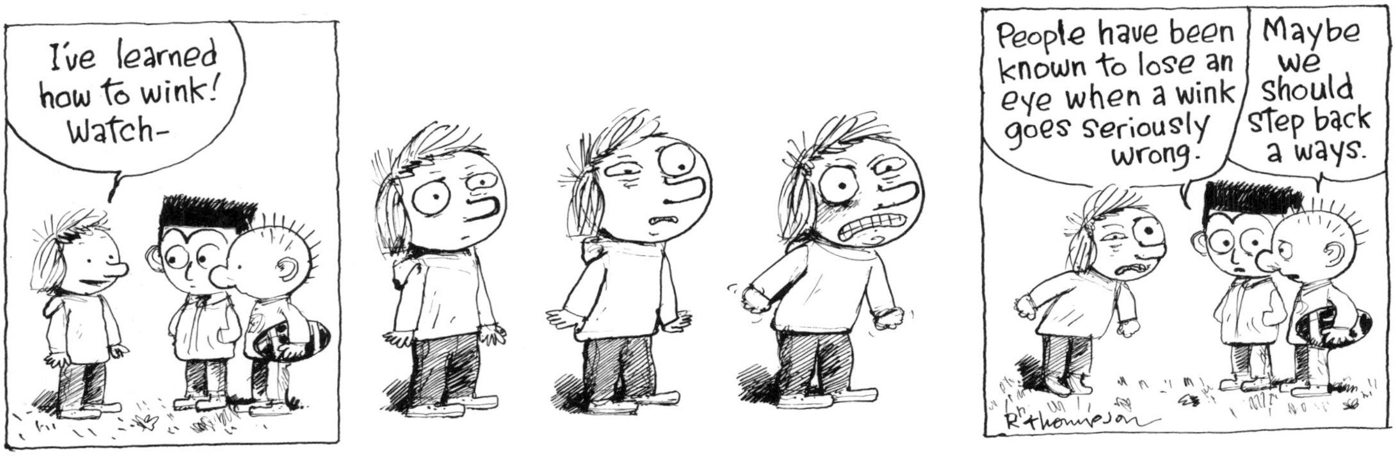
I've learned how to wink! Watch-
People have been known to lose an eye when a wink goes seriously wrong.
Maybe we should step back a ways.

Pop!

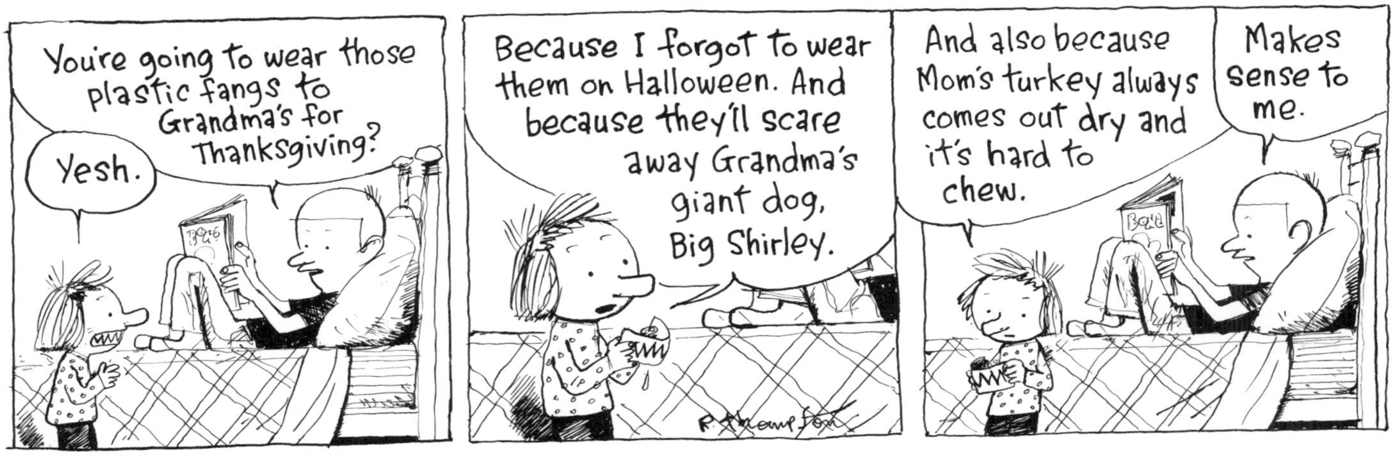
You're going to wear those plastic fangs to Grandma's for Thanksgiving?
Yesh.
Because I forgot to wear them on Halloween. And because they'll scare away Grandma's giant dog, Big Shirley.
And also because Mom's turkey always comes out dry and it's hard to chew.
Makes sense to me.

Grandma goes feral again.

I like the idea that Grandma's house is layered and piled with slag heaps of stuff, some of it slowly becoming semitoxic.

Emphasizing the right words is a tricky business. Like too many exclamation points, too much emphasis loses impact and everything turns into a shouting match. Choosing the right form of emphasis is tricky, too, as there are many of them and each marks a different change of tone. You've got the simple underline, the double and multiple underline, the wiggly underline, the boldface, the drop-shadow block caps, and on and on. They're like the forte and piano markings in music notation.

Grandma's beet casserole. Only last year, Grandma was turning away any dish with beets. Is no one taking care of continuity on this strip?

189

Petey's taste in comics is often pretty severe and depressing. Toad zombies are no doubt some scathing commentary on our consumerist culture.

This may be the first time this issue has been addressed in a comic strip, making any second time completely unnecessary.

Expanded somewhat, this would make a great Beloved Annual Christmas TV Special.

As drawn, it looks more like Dill is mackin', or truckin', than moseyin'.

At some point in the strip's first year, I realized that Petey had no milieu, no friends, or life, really. Somehow, this is what I came up with.

Learning to wink is important at around four years old. Learning to cross your eyes is, too, and about as difficult.

This form is called the Silent Penultimate Panel. The next to last panel is used as a pause in the joke, where a reaction is given time to slowly register. Here, Mrs. Otterloop uses it to smack herself in the kisser.

You've got a new Christmas sweater!

Viola's balloon in the second panel is an instance of increasing the underlinings to indicate a crescendo. Just a technical note for those who're paying attention.

When flushing ice cubes doesn't work, be a nuisance.

The whole Santa thing at some point seems a little creepy. Parents talk him up like he's so great, but I think Santa's got some personal problems. But please don't tell anybody I said so, especially the kids.